PENGUIN BOOKS

ONLY A GAME?

Eamon Dunphy is an Irish writer and broadcaster. He played professional soccer in England for seventeen years. He is also the author of *Unforgettable Fire: The Story of U2*, *More Than a Job?* (with Roger Titford), *More Than a Game* and *A Strange Kind of Glory: Sir Matt Busby and Manchester United*.

Peter Ball wrote extensively on sport, especially cricket and football, for many publications, including *Time Out*, where he started the magazine's sports section in 1973, *The Times* and the *London Daily News*. He collaborated on and edited a number of books on sport and sportsmen. Peter Ball died in November 1997.

EAMON DUNPHY

Only a Game?

The Diary of a
Professional Footballer

SECOND EDITION

Edited, with a postscript, by Peter Ball
With a preface by Brian Glanville

PENGUIN BOOKS

PENGUIN BOOKS

Published by the Penguin Group
Penguin Books Ltd, 27 Wrights Lane, London w8 5TZ, England
Penguin Putnam Inc., 375 Hudson Street, New York, New York 10014, USA
Penguin Books Australia Ltd, Ringwood, Victoria, Australia
Penguin Books Canada Ltd, 10 Alcorn Avenue, Toronto, Ontario, Canada M4V 3B2
Penguin Books (NZ) Ltd, Private Bag 102902, NSMC, Auckland, New Zealand

Penguin Books Ltd, Registered Offices: Harmondsworth, Middlesex, England

First published by Viking 1976
Second edition published 1986
Published in Penguin Books 1987
10 9 8 7 6 5 4

Printed in England by Clays Ltd, St Ives plc

To the good pro

Contents

Acknowledgements

Acknowledgements may be boring to read. And there is no way that one can convey adequately in such a short space the amount of help received. But nonetheless, however inadequate this might appear, we would like to express our thanks to the many people who helped to make this book. First, to Sarah Ball and Sandra Dunphy, who put up with many lost weekends and vast telephone bills in its cause, as well as providing encouragement and criticism in equal and appropriate proportions. To Chris Lightbown, without whose energy and enthusiasm the book might never have got off the ground. To Frank Keating and Brian Glanville, whose interest and practical help gave us much needed encouragement. To Sue Buckholt, who transcribed and typed some of the material. To Millwall F.C. for allowing us to reproduce an excerpt from the club programme. And to all the others too numerous to mention who showed interest. Finally, to someone we have never met: Jim Bouton, an American baseball star, whose diary of one season, *Ball Four*, suggested the format for this book. If this book is even half as good as his, all the people who have helped can feel they've contributed to something worthwile. If it isn't, then the blame is ours.

Preface (1976)

Eamon Dunphy's diary is the best and most authentic memoir by a professional footballer about his sport that I have yet read. It is infinitely removed from the 'ghosted' pap which, with its endless banalities and disingenuousness, has so long been inflicted on us. Not that I feel we have been at last introduced to the 'true' football. There are as many truths about the game as there are about any other widely practised activity, and Dunphy's own truth would clearly vary in accordance with the point in his career.

In this case, the point is a somewhat low one. Millwall, at the time, were not doing well, so the narrative tends to be tart. There is a latent feeling that not only Millwall but Dunphy himself, by then in his late twenties, have somehow missed the boat. An international footballer of skill and vision, he had still to play regularly in the First Division, where he surely belonged. There is disillusionment with directors, managers, coaches, journalists, referees, fellow players, much dejection, little joy. Yet clearly it is hope that has soured, idealism that has been disappointed. Though no attempt is made to disguise the pro footballer's endemic paranoia, it is also plain that Dunphy knows how he feels the game should be played and approached, and is the more put out when it's exploited and distorted.

Let us be grateful for what we have, even if it would have been better still to have had Dunphy as tyro, Dunphy in his other existences at Manchester United, York, Charlton, Reading. He has had the courage, as Arthur Miller wrote elsewhere, to let himself be known. The acquaintance is rewarding.

Brian Glanville

Introduction (1986)

When I wrote *Only a Game?* I dedicated it to the good pro – not to my children, Mum and Dad, my wife or my brother, all of whom I dearly loved, but to a character who to them and indeed to the world at large must have seemed as abstract as other fictional creations. To me the good pro was real. He was the man I wanted to be, the man I wanted around me when I went to work in the Second Division of the Football League between 1966 and 1973.

I believe the good pro was the true hero of professional sport. He is not necessarily a great player, or even the best player in the team, although he can be both. His goodness has to do not just with his talent but also with his spiritual state. The good pro is a trier – not one of those despised young automatons that pass for midfield players these days, all sweat and crunching tackles, but a much nobler embodiment of sporting virtue. The good pro accepts responsibility – both his and, when the going gets tough, yours. Most of his virtues are invisible from the stands and terraces. When his team is defending, he is alert, tracking his opponent and denying *his* man time and space, while always on the lookout for trouble elsewhere. If you are in the shit, have given *your* man that crucial extra yard or two, have lost your concentration for a minute, the good pro will often rescue you, leaving his man to get in a saving tackle or making what looks to the crowd like a simple interception. He is woven into the fabric of every good side and every great side too. When you are attacking, he makes himself available to receive the ball – not just when you are 2–0 up at home, or when, with nothing to lose, you are 2–0 down away from home, but when it takes a bit of moral courage, when you are struggling to make the breakthrough in front of your own impatient fans or when you are hanging on with five minutes to go away from home. He will make the run, get that vital touch in the box, go for a return pass instead of holding back. In attack or defence, at home or away, in January mud, April wind or August sunshine, every game is a test and there are so many ways to cheat, to walk away from your responsibility to the team. The good pro never does. He is sometimes knackered, often in despair, but never out of the ball game, never on the missing list.

He is my man. He is the footballer's footballer, the sportsman's sportsman. He may not be 'what the game is about', if it is about something more, something grander, called, perhaps, inspiration. But his integrity, his nobility of spirit, his dedication to duty and his commitment to cause are what the game was largely about for this journeyman pro. Looking back now at Millwall, the nearly men of so many Second Division years, I think of 'the lads'. They were, I am certain, the best men I will ever know – maybe not innately so but by virtue of the work they did. Sport, even in the Second Division, perhaps particularly in the Second Division of those years which was full of hard men like Bobby Kellard and Willie Carlin and good players like Trevor Francis, Keith Weller and Graeme Souness, was good for you, made a man of you and, if you were to survive and prosper, a good pro.

Maybe we weren't all that great to begin with, but after eight seasons in the trench that was the Second Division we were enriched. If you cheated, fell below the good pro standard, you were found out – by your opponents, by your team-mates *and* by yourself.

Our lives were like other men's lives except for the game. We had children, mortgages, cars that didn't start, wives that bitched, overdrafts and gardens that needed tending. But those were other people's realities; ours was the game. Were we in the side? Was the side winning? Was I as fit as I should be? Would the wound heal for Saturday? Could the manager get *his* act together? Would we get a result this week? These were our obsessions.

Saturday was the day. On that day's result and performance

everything else depended. How different from the real world, where creative accountancy, a deal or a compromise could save the day, where trade unions, professional associations, political parties, religious sects or self-perpetuating class systems could protect cheats and hide their inadequacies from the world and themselves. In sport, in the Second Division, there was no hiding place. The world applied different standards when judging you. The cheats or simple inadequates of other walks of life could come to the Den and apply to our work a set of judgemental criteria they wouldn't have dreamed of applying on Monday morning. Fuck them. And fuck the journalists who confirmed their prejudices.

Today when I reflect on the lads, I do so from *my* seat in the press-box. I have made a go of life in the real world. Now I am among them, the type of people who watch sport and presume they know what is going on out there, the type of people who run the world, who regard sport as, well, a simple thing, only a game, the type of people the sportsman secretly despises.

There are good pros in the real world, but being a good pro is not a prerequisite to worldly success, not by a long chalk. For the most part, the values espoused by the good pro will get you into trouble out here. I travel with them, work with them, eat with them and listen to them. I sit in the weekly news conference and watch them posing, copping out when they are 2–0 down, when they are 2–0 up and in all conceivable ways regardless of the scoreline. In the real world the thing to be is smart. It wouldn't have been enough at Millwall – or even Hartlepool!

Almost a decade after leaving I understand better than ever that what distinguishes sport from the real world around it is the degree to which the sportsman has to have values and has to adhere to them. Ethics matter everywhere, but in sport they matter more than anywhere else. In a darkening world where the shadows of violence, political expediency, materialism and junk culture grow ever longer, sport as it is practised by its good pros remains a bastion of decency, a place where virtue is rewarded and cheating exposed.

Living in the real world rams that home. Sometimes I intervene to make the point and invariably a powerful and successful cheat will put me in my place. 'Dear Eamon, life is not a football game,' he will sneer to murmurs of agreement from the assembled company.

Only a Game? is an attempt to convey something of the reality of professional soccer. Sadly, the reality it conveys is grim. What is recorded is the bitter end of a journey that was not always bitter, that for a time at least seemed as if it might end triumphantly with us achieving our goal – promotion to the First Division. Millwall is the only London club not to have made it to the First Division. A couple of seasons before this book was written we failed by a single point to make club history. Norwich and Birmingham went up and Millwall finished third, our highest ever Football League position and one that would, ironically, have been good enough to lure the Liverpools and Manchester Uniteds to the Den after the League was restructured a few years later. That was a good professional team in which I am proud to have played.

The team that nearly made it in 1971–2 was a good pro's team, a truer reflection of the people in it, and their values, than the side falling apart in the pages of *Only a Game?* Benny Fenton created both, and if *Only a Game?* has a hero, in retrospect it is Benny. One of the things the book succeeds in conveying is football's irrationality. Its depiction of Benny as a weak man is proof of this, for he was far more than that. He was a decent, civilized, intelligent football man, and he was also a victim of the game's passions, of young men's arrogance, of terrace prejudice and boardroom stupidity. When I reflect on my part in his downfall, I feel guilty. I feel worse: I am ashamed of my bloody-minded insensitivity to the difficulties he faced managing the club. Like all footballers, I thought only of myself. (Yes, I acknowledge the conflict here between the good pro ethic and self. The contradiction is easily resolved by understanding that all loyalties and commitments to the team are conditional, conditional upon you being in it!)

Benny got off to a bad start when he took over as manager of Millwall in May 1966. We had just won promotion from the Third Division, but the management team of Billy Gray and Bill Dodgin who had led us to that success resigned because the directors wouldn't provide money for the better quality players we would need in the Second Division. Benny was hired to replace Gray and

Dodgin, who left as martyrs. Players and supporters alike saw Benny Fenton as a boardroom man and, on account of the wheeler-dealer reputation that preceded him, as someone who would gladly pursue the penny-pinching policies the Millwall board was notorious for.

The team he inherited was good, by Third Division standards. Alex Stepney in goal added a touch of class to a defence that was rough, experienced and nerveless. But Stepney was leaving for Chelsea. Would the board spend the money they got from Chelsea on some Second Division players?

That was the question that Millwall supporters pondered on as the side that was now Benny Fenton's took its place in the Second Division. The benefit of any doubt was given neither to the board of directors nor to Benny. The real villain of this piece was one Mickey Purser of Purser Car Sales on the Old Kent Road. Mickey, or the Chairman, as Benny was forced to address him, was Mister Big, the majority shareholder. It didn't help Benny's cause that he was seen as Mickey's boy.

The team Benny inherited was all but unbeatable at home. When you looked around the Den it wasn't hard to see why. The place was distinctly lacking in ambiance. Having wound their way through a maze of narrow streets off the Old Kent Road, visiting teams would draw up outside what looked like a derelict factory. Here, grey was the primary colour. What wasn't grey needed a coat of paint. The pitch was tight – and bumpy. The visitors' dressing-room was dark and narrow, as welcoming as a British Rail loo. Only good teams and brave players survived their introduction to the Lions' Den. And even some of them changed their minds when the game kicked off. At that stage visiting players discovered that the fans were as hostile as the decor. Even small Millwall crowds made a fearsome noise, which chilled the bones of many a Northern hard man who'd come to London believing Southerners were soft. This was the wrong part of London.

To us the Den was home, its wit always good for a laugh, its passion often worth a goal or two. If the game was boring the crowd would amuse itself by picking on some unfortunate player – home or away – whose every desperate lunge would draw roars of derision. Sometimes this unique gathering would parody itself. If the home team's efforts were particularly fruitless, mock passion could be conjured up on the terraces.

Coming to this raucous dockland music hall, a smart manager might have decided to play to the audience. He might have decided to build a side likely to respond to the rough and ready atmosphere, a side that might in turn draw a response from the dockers on the terraces. Benny, displaying courage that belied his dodgy image, chose instead to go for class.

The old promotion team did well in its first season in the Second Division. We survived comfortably, but were never going to achieve anything more than that. Having consolidated, Benny set about building his own team. He was a superb judge of a player and a shrewd transfer market operator. The players he brought to the club over the next few years were a subtle but determined challenge to the Millwall tradition. They had one thing in common: all of them could play. Men like Keith Weller, Dennis Burnett, Derek Possee, Gordon Bolland, Brian Clark, Barry Bridges, Bryan Brown, Frank Saul and, yes, even Gordon Hill were good footballers. (No, *not* Gordon Hill.) They were unlikely to scare opponents to death but would instead try and play them off the park. Benny also bought Bryan King from Chelmsford to play in goal and converted Barry Kitchener from full-back to centre-half. And kept me, in defiance of many on the terraces and in the boardroom.

Yes, he 'liked a bit of class', as he would sometimes smilingly confide to me, off the field as well. Benny was an East Ender from across the river. He liked to look the part and was always smartly dressed, showing plenty of cuff, with hair neatly groomed. I can still see him now after a particularly satisfying performance by 'his boys', standing in front of the dressing-room mirror, comb in hand, readying himself for a triumphant boardroom entrance. He was a nice man, a cut above us and more than a cut above those bastards upstairs. And he was a refined man, the passion buried beneath the smart suit and the crombie overcoat. He liked, he would admit shyly in unguarded moments, 'a bit of Strauss, a drop of nice wine'; his hobby was bowls. He never raised his voice and he hated the gutter press to whom we would run with our tales of discontent.

They in turn hated him and were always eager to sustain the image of Benny the con-man.

To some extent he was, if not a con-man, a subversive in our football world. He had to be. This was English football after Ramsey, when Leeds United were *the* team and Arsenal, under Bertie Mee and Don Howe, would soon be doing the double, with a team featuring Peter Storey. This was the Second Division whose traditional hardness had been reinforced by the inclusion in every side of Peter Storey/Norman Hunter clones, complete in every detail except talent. On top of everything, this was Millwall, a club whose time might be said to have arrived. And here was Benny Fenton, suspected spiv, trying to win promotion with a footballing side, a really good footballing side in which unlike, say, West Ham, the good footballers weren't afraid to sweat. With a good PR man Benny might have become Ron Greenwood! He, we, failed narrowly. It was a glorious failure in its small way: it was as near as Benny or I or any of the lads would get to being really famous.

It is in this context that *Only a Game?* should be read. And it is in this context – the context of glorious failure – that Benny Fenton should properly be remembered. As the book predicts, he got the sack in the end. He came back in various roles with Charlton Athletic, the club he once captained as a classy, extrovert wing-half, but that was only a matter of earning a 'few bob'.

They should build a monument to Benny at Cold Blow Lane. It is their tragedy that they don't know why. Football is dead in England today for many reasons, not the least of which is the game's failure to find work for intelligent football men whose moment in the playing arena has passed. Benny was one such. There were others: Nicholson, Cullis, Ramsey, Busby, Arthur Rowe, Blanchflower – men of character and wisdom who were treated like common servants when their time in the dressing-room was served. As a consequence you have the English game we see today. For all the time that I have known it, football's best men have been subversives.

We get a Christmas card from Boston, Lincs., each year, so I know that Gordon Bolland is alive and well up there. I haven't seen him for about fifteen years. I am not sentimental by nature, but I would love to spend a weekend with the lads, have a laugh about the past, find out what they are doing now and how, if at all, they have changed. Old footballers never die, they simply scatter on the four winds, usually ending up in their home town. Unlike old soldiers, we don't have reunions. We should.

Billy Neill still works for Millwall on the commercial staff. Like a lot of old footballers, he suffers from arthritis. I met Bryan King in Oslo last year: 'Kingy' is coaching a Norwegian Fourth Division club. We got drunk together and reminisced. Alan Dorney retrained as a bricklayer, I believe, and took a 'proper' job. The last I heard of Harry Cripps, he was surviving – coaching at Crystal Palace. I met Derek Possee in Vancouver, where he was at the time an out-of-work coach. Keith Weller is also coaching, in North America. Somebody told me that Keith's young son died tragically – vague news of old comrades, friends from another time, another life almost.

When we trekked up and down England's motorways we thought it would last forever, this extended adolescence. Alas, we got old, our legs lost their strength when we were still young, in our early thirties. It is a rather sad if predictable postscript to the story of our team that some of the lads who played so loyally for the club never got the treatment they deserved. Alan Dorney was denied his entitlement to a decent testimonial and Barry Kitchener was messed around as youth team coach.

There is no true club ethos in pro football. There never was. It is therefore ironic in 1986 to hear clubs bitching about the cavalier way modern footballers exercise the freedom of contract that has revolutionized the player/club relationship. In the past you could be a great player and never become rich; now you can get rich without being a great player. Equity has never been achieved and never will be now.

One of sport's saddest sounds is the whine of yesterday's men making unfavourable comparisons between the awful present and *their* glorious past. Oh, dear, not those old buggers again, I used to think when some 'short-back-and-sides' merchant was wheeled on in the sixties to tell us about the horrors of the modern game. Much of what the Stan Matthews generation had to say was nonsense. In retrospect, the British game in the sixties and early seventies was enjoying a Golden Age, a historic phase in which technical excellence and physical fitness combined to produce the best footballers of the century. Unlike Stan Matthews, Bobby Charlton faced defenders who were as fit and mobile as he was, men like Dave Mackay, Bobby Moore and Norman Hunter.

However conscious one is of the irritation to be felt when confronted with other men's 'good old days', however reluctant one is to indulge the beast nostalgia, yet the truth of English football in 1986 is inescapable: the game has 'gone'. It possesses only one great player – Bryan Robson. Anyone who can pass and control the ball like, say Peter Reid is held in awe now. If you don't possess these basic skills you can still play in the First Division – for Sheffield Wednesday. What has happened to football since *Only a Game?* was written doesn't bear thinking about. Then, on any winter Saturday you could see George Best, Bobby Charlton, John Giles, Billy Bremner, Bobby Moore, Alan Ball, Martin Peters, Denis Law, Colin Bell; Robert Maxwell was merely a publisher; Ken Bates was a failed fringe banker; and Lawrie McMenemy was managing Doncaster Rovers. If I were to write the book again in 1986 I think I would remove the question mark.

Eamon Dunphy

I Pre-Season

25 July

The first day. An interesting day. You leave in April tired, cynical, a bit disillusioned. Now you are really happy when you come back. People are always happy to come back. On the first day, you have the photo call, and everyone compares sun tans, and tells lies about the girls they've had. You don't really talk about the season today. It's a day for acclimatization: getting used to seeing everyone again, and looking at the new faces.

One of the funny things is when you first go into the ground, and you see the pitch with no posts and no lines drawn.

You are very conscious, though, underneath all the clowning, that you have come back to work. People think that the season lasts from the middle of August to the end in April. But it really starts today.

26 July

Today we went to Peak Frean's sports ground on the Sidcup bypass. And it was hard. The first day is always hard. But it is not the hardest. The first day you feel exuberant, you want to run and run, and your legs are tired. But it's the second day. Then you are knackered. You've got a reaction from the first day.

And then you slip into it all so quickly again. You spend the morning working, from half past ten until 12.00, then have some lunch, then work again in the afternoon. You finish about four, and you are really knackered. Yet it is a marvellous spiritual feeling. You have worked hard, and are cleansed. I think that footballers, and all athletic people, when they go away in the summer and eat and drink too much, and stay up too late, have this tremendous guilt. Pre-season training gets rid of that guilt.

There is nothing more exhilarating than coming home feeling tired, and sitting down and feeling pure in a way that you never do in the season. The tension of the season is not there yet; the sense of battle has not arisen yet.

There is a great deal of good-natured banter. The atmosphere of a pre-season training camp is idyllic. You are away from the ground, it's secluded, and you feel as if you are in the country. It's sunny, and you're happy. The team has not been picked yet. So there is no competition, and everybody feels they are eligible. The divisions have not been drawn yet. Relationships are very very good. Guys you haven't liked before, and who you will probably hate again later in the season, seem all right in this kind of atmosphere.

The manager is very happy. No problems, no battles yet. All the theories sound great. Benny strolls among us, benign, fond of his players, seeing us in our nicest light.

There is a great feeling of unity at this time. Obviously reserves are worried. Last year I was worried whether I would be in the team; I had finished the season before just in the team. And if you are in that situation of being on the fringe of the team, you are watching everything. You watch the manager's face for expression, for any clue as to how he feels about you. For the first two weeks, it is all work, no mention of teams yet. I waited and waited until he picked the team. I wasn't in it, so I left. I walked out in the middle of pre-season training. I had worried about it all that summer, and when the blow came, I couldn't take it. It was too much; it was unbearable really. It would have been the first time in my career that I did not kick off in the first team. You work so hard in pre-season training; you really kill yourself. And you do it with one thing in mind. The first day of the season. If you are not in the team it has all been a waste. It invalidates the whole thing.

But that worry is for the future. For the moment there's just hard work, and good group feeling.

27 July

We went to Peak Frean's again today. It was really hot, in the eighties, and we were all feeling the aching limbs of yesterday. And it was hard. So we went over as normal to the pub across the bypass for lunch. It was the regular lunch; orange juice and salad. And because we were going back to train again in the afternoon we had the normal rule of one glass of orange juice only. You can't train if you're full up with liquid.

Of course you always try and dive in before Benny, or Lawrie, or Billy Neill get in there, and grab a glass so that you can have two instead of one. Everyone does it. But there are varying degrees of indiscipline. And one or two of the fat buggers were having three or four extra glasses. You can't train properly if you are drinking that much. At this stage it seems unimportant. But it isn't. Because if you can't discipline yourself over a small thing like that, you've got no hope over anything more serious.

We've got a couple of new lads: free-transfers from Arsenal and Spurs. I spoke to the lad from Arsenal today. Normally new lads, particularly ones who haven't done anything before, are a bit quiet. They like to feel their way in. When I was that age, first-teamers only spoke to you to tell you to clean their boots or whatever. But this lad was completely unabashed. 'I've only come here for first-team football,' he said.

Oh well, we'd all better watch out, then. Because he meant it.

1 August

We've been doing a lot of work against the stop-watch. Lawrie – the coach – has rigged up all sorts of graphs, and times and tests. We'd all been suspicious that it was a load of fannying, and we got conclusive proof this morning.

We were doing these sixty-yard sprints against the clock. Kingy, one of the fastest runners in the club, went first, and got clocked in at 8.1 secs. Harry went last. He's the slowest person in the club, and he gets clocked in at 7.9. Lawrie might have got away with it, but Kingy spotted it straight away. He went mad. 'Lawrie, how can that fat so-and-so be 0.2 of a second quicker than me?'

We all fell about, but it confirmed our suspicions. It's funny because we'd had this feeling about him. And we were looking for conclusive proof. Now that little, almost insignificant, incident had confirmed it for us. So Lawrie is standing there, mumbling 'I must have pressed it wrong.' Of course then everyone is diving in, shouting 'You must have pressed it wrong for my time too.'

It's a question of credibility. If you're training against a watch, you've got to know that it's right. The same thing could happen to Malcolm Allison, but you would never think to question his credibility. If you noticed the discrepancy, your tendency would be to keep quiet about it. But when there's a credibility gap to start with, that's the kind of thing you jump on. Everyone was going around muttering 'Told you so.'

I'm not convinced that you really are fitter after three weeks than one. And that's what the stop-watch is all about. Proving it. Of course, the training staff are always terrified that you aren't getting fitter. So they devise all these schedules to test you. To reassure themselves that you are getting fitter.

You can get badly caught. Because if you dive in and give your best the first week, like the naive and the honest do, you might not show any improvement a week later. And they are always looking for improvement in your times. You often get the cynical old pro who will go very steady the first week, top it up a bit the second week, and really go flat out the last week. If he ever goes flat out, that is.

It's hard to gauge your own fitness. In pre-season you get worried. You start thinking that you aren't doing this right, not doing that right. So the stop-watch is a valuable means of reassurance for the players too. But it must be held by a credible man.

2 August

Lawrie's graph created a lovely incident this morning. He'd been keeping this graph of our times in sprints, which he had put up in the dressing-room. After yesterday's mess-ups, everyone was off Lawrie, his stop-watch and his graph, which was a real amateurish job anyway – just a page of foolscap. So yesterday Kingy and Brownie took it off the wall and put it on the ceiling 'so it would be more readable'. Then they took it off the ceiling, and put it in the wastepaper basket. Then they took it out and played football with it, and they eventually threw it in the nettles round the back.

This morning Lawrie came in looking for his graph, and his face was like thunder. He was not speaking to anyone. We think Lawrie is a fanny merchant. But he plays the role – honest pro, straightforward guy, loves the game, loves doing the right things.

Anyhow he got us all together and said 'Who is the lousy, stinking yellow-livered bastard who took the graph off the wall?' The lads were sitting there quietly killing themselves. I was sitting at the front, and Lawrie was looking at me suspiciously. Before he had this meeting he had asked me and Kingy if we knew anything about it. I had said I didn't.

Benny was hovering in the distance. He knew what had happened. Was he laughing inwardly too?

'Come on. Own up in front of your mates. Be a man. At least you can be a man, and own up.'

So he was looking round. And the lads! You should have seen their faces! We were all trying desperately not to laugh.

Then he said 'I'm going to tell you something. Me and my kid; my kid did that graph! My kid sat in the garden on Sunday afternoon, and he did that graph for YOU! And he was proud to think he was doing something for the professional footballers of Millwall – his heroes. And we worked on it all afternoon. He was so proud. And now some bastard has taken it down off the wall. And that's my kid's, MY KID'S!'

I couldn't see Kingy. All the messers – Kingy, Gordon, Brownie – were at the back, and I had sat at the front, not knowing what was coming.

'I'm inviting you to come up to my room after training, and we'll have it out man to man. Because let me tell you this: my kids are more important to me than this job. I can always get another job.'

All the time he was saying this in a broad Scots accent. I was really tempted to say 'Kingy, stand up'. They are two nutters, and the confrontation would have been incredible. It would have been the fight to end all fights.

Anyway, no one owned up. So he said 'That's me finished! No more graphs!'

He was thinking 'You're not getting any more of those lovely graphs you like so much.' And we were thinking 'Thank Christ for that!'

He really tried to put us through it in training afterwards. Really tried to make us suffer, but we were all breaking up laughing.

It was outrageous for Lawrie to react in that way. We hadn't known his kid had done the graph, and he should not expose his kid to that sort of risk anyway. He stuck it up with two bits of sellotape. I know that Chelsea have graphs, but this was a real amateur job.

3 August

My birthday. I am twenty-eight; getting on, getting a tiny bit worried. This is going to be the big season. It has to be: there may not be many more. Twenty-eight – the age when insecurity like a slowly descending fog appears on the horizon. One is conscious of little things – the apprentices begin to seem absurdly young, you call them 'son' now, and yet it doesn't seem so long since older players addressed you the same way. Players you played with or against are getting jobs as managers, or retiring. The manager begins to consult you more often. 'What do you think of this and that?' It's flattering, of course – you have grown up, but you are growing old, too, at least in football terms.

You talk more of babies, and not so much of birds. You begin to wonder what is coming from the Provident Fund, about a testimonial, sometimes at night about retirement – the end. How much longer will you spend your summers in this idyllic way, dreaming of glory? Of course, you reassure yourself that this is your prime. It's a shock to realize how rapid the descent is from pinnacle to valley.

I have from time to time pondered on all of those fears, but today I watched Harry Cripps, at thirty-two the oldest player on the staff, exuberant as ever and enjoying it all as if he was fifteen again. Harry is a unique yet strangely reassuring figure. A truly great professional, not particularly gifted, except for boundless enthusiasm and love for football and the life we lead. A seemingly simple, yet I find a tantalizing, complex figure. He is at once selfish, good-natured, devious and honest – but always lovable.

4 August

Today we had our first full-scale practice game. Of course you can never tell, of course practice games don't prove very much, etc., etc. But it all went well. There is no way it isn't going to go well this season.

And that was after a bad start too. Because Dennis Burnett, the club captain, didn't turn up for the game. That was a real downer to start on. He's been wanting to leave the club for some time now; he is in dispute with them at the moment, and has not yet re-signed for this season.

Messing about like this has always been his way of putting pressure on. Or perhaps he is just sulking. Anyway, we demanded of Benny that this time he take some action against Dennis. He's always been soft about these things in the past. Benny isn't really a disciplinarian. He believes in coaxing people, almost seducing them. He thinks that you get more co-operation that way, which on the whole you do, but you also get people who do not respond. And Dennis has never really responded. This is a big season for us, and we need everyone giving everything. So we demanded that this time Benny take action. Which he has agreed to.

6 August

This morning, when Dennis came in, Benny was waiting for him. He was stalking, waiting, and as soon as Dennis got out of his car Benny went for him then and there. The explanation, as it turned out, was that Dennis's baby had meningitis. Benny said he should have phoned and said what was wrong. And the upshot was that Dennis was told to go home and was suspended for a week.

This was a blow to us, because we had been the ones who urged Benny to take action, and now we were worried that this was the wrong time to take the action.

When Dennis had gone, and we had got changed, Benny called a meeting. He explained to us all that he had finally taken action. He was willing to take action this time because of the previous year: I had walked out, Barry Bridges had been in dispute with the club, and Possee had wanted to get away. That all resulted in us being bottom of the League after two months, and we were all determined that it would not happen again.

It was a unique atmosphere; there we all were in one group, twenty-two players, two coaches and a manager. He asked for opinions when he finished; had we anything to say? And there was a kind of worried silence. People in one sense understood his action, in other senses were terribly worried.

I suggested that perhaps this was the wrong time to hit Dennis, and that when it came to matters of family like this, your duty was to your family rather than to the game. One or two people agreed, and then we had a debate on it that lasted until quarter to twelve. It was then half past ten.

It was a very frank, open and democratic exchange, with everyone having a say, including the apprentices.

In the debate, I was the first one to speak because I felt I was in a good position to defend Dennis since I had not been particularly friendly with him for many years. He has got a strong personality, and so have I, and we did not really like each other very much; although recently we had begun to get on well. When Dennis was the sweeper, he thought I could not play, that I was just a useless sixpenny ball-player. That changed when he came and joined me playing in midfield. When you share a job with somebody in football, a relationship develops between you, an understanding that you do not have with players doing a totally different job. If you are just knocking a ball between you, on a training ground, a relationship develops between you. It's a form of expression – you are communicating as much as if you are making love to somebody. If you take two players who work together in midfield, say, they will know each other through football as intimately as any two lovers. That would apply to Giles and Bremner, for example. It's a very close relationship you build up when you are resolving problems together, trying to create situations together. It's an unspoken relationship, but your movements speak, your game speaks. The kind of ball you give each other, the kind of passes you give each other, the kind of situations you set up together, speak for you. You don't necessarily become closer in a social sense, but you develop a close unspoken understanding. This is what happened with Dennis and me. Working in midfield had brought us considerably closer, although not as buddies.

So I felt I was qualified to speak up in his defence, also because I had been the one most anxious that action should be taken. I had felt that the way Dennis was going about it was wrong; when I had had a dispute, I'd been open and frank about it. I had said, 'Look, I'm going.'

But we felt that Dennis, not having turned up on Saturday morning, would come in on Monday morning, and everything would be all right again. But then he would go off again when he felt like it. That was his form of protest.

Kitch agreed with me, but Alf Wood didn't. He thought that Dennis had a problem and we should all sympathize with him, but nevertheless he should have phoned the club. He felt the suspension should stand.

Benny felt that if he changed his decision in front of the players, it would show weakness. And so somebody would try it again some time in the future.

Here again, I felt qualified to speak up because I have challenged him more than anybody probably. If I could say that I would not consider it weakness, then it would show he was not likely to have any trouble on this.

I asked Harry, who is Dennis's closest friend and business partner, what he thought. And Harry, in his unique way, is loyal first to football and his own position in it, and he said he would abide by the decision taken by the club; which was really a way of saying 'No comment.'

I got angry at this, and said, 'For Christ's sake, don't you feel *anything*?' And he said 'When I come inside this club, I come to work; when I go out of the gate, it is a different situation altogether. Although I am closest to Dennis, I am not prepared to go any further than that.' That is the way it is with Harry, and I think Dennis knows it.

Finally, Benny agreed that he would phone Dennis, and that Harry and I would accompany him to the phone. Harry phoned Dennis, and said that we had had a meeting and that Benny was here, and wanted to speak to him.

Benny got on, and said 'Come back for lunch, and we'll forget about it.' I think this was the right way because Millwall is a small club, and we pride ourselves on our family atmosphere and our closeness; and I think this situation was one where we should forget the differences we had with Dennis and rally round him.

Anyway, he came back for lunch, and we were all very relieved, including him. I was glad he was back: I think he is a very important member of the side.

This was all crucial, because if we had not had that meeting, then Dennis would have been suspended for a week, he would have lost the captaincy, and there would probably have been no possibility of him playing for Millwall again. So that exercise in democracy worked. I don't think there are many clubs in the country where it would have worked.

After that, my respect for Benny zoomed upwards. I thought he acted strongly, whatever his reasons were. He responded to the majority wishes.

7 August

Lawrie has not got a very flexible, or wide, vocabulary, to say the least. He uses words like 'motivation' and 'aspect'. He's always telling the lads about this and that 'aspect'. He starts off by saying 'There are various aspects we can work out', which is fair enough; then he says 'This is one aspect', and he'll go on to use 'aspect' half a dozen times. He says things like 'This aspect has gone wrong.' He uses the word 'motivate' as well. He says things like 'We're not getting motivated this morning.'

He talks about this Hungarian coaching book he read; this great Hungarian coach has given 365 training routines, one for every day of the year. In a moment of weakness, he made the mistake of telling me about this, and I told the lads. He's going on about this really fantastic book he is reading, and then coming out with these really incredible routines; they have no relation to football at all. They are just pure exercises in teaching.

The test of a good coach, to people in the FA, is how well they set up an exercise, and how well they teach it. That's it; you are a good coach if you can do that well. When you take your coaching course, it is how well you set up what you are trying to teach, and how well you teach it, talk through it. Nothing to do with the value the players are getting out of it.

8 August

You look forward to a five-a-side at the end of a hard morning's work. It's great. You get the ball and away you go and enjoy yourselves for the first time that morning. But Lawrie's had this thing recently about conditioned five-a-side games. Which means you always have a restriction put on you. You can only pass the ball forward, or only have two touches, that kind of thing. Every morning he's been giving us these conditioned games, which spoils the enjoyment. It makes them difficult too. So we had been getting really fed up.

This morning he came up with a corker. You couldn't pass the ball until you had beaten a man. Now this was impossible. All you had to do to stop the other team doing anything was to run away from them, so they couldn't beat you. Of course it became a farce.

In that kind of situation most players will do it until they get a reaction from the senior players – Harry, Dennis or me. I don't wait for reactions. I just jacked it in, and went and stood in goal. But Harry is one of those guys, if the trainer says 'Eat shit' Harry would eat it. As long as it was official, Harry would do it. And all of a sudden, Harry, of all unlikely people, picked up the ball, and said 'That's enough of that. We're playing two-touch or the normal five-a-side.'

Lawrie stood there. I think he realized he'd gone too far this time. Because if Harry reacted against it, it must have been really impossible. So he shrugged his shoulders, looked hurt, and accepted it. If Dennis or I had picked the ball up, Lawrie could have had a right go at us, as we are recognized trouble-makers. But Harry had never been known to rebel in his life.

So at last we got our normal five-a-side game.

It's funny the way coaches have this thing about conditioned games, and all these weird theories they get out of the *FA Coaching Manual*. It's the same in every club. John Giles was telling me they'd had the same trouble with their coaches at Leeds, and they had all had to go and see Revie to get it stopped.

Some of the things coaches do, some of the games they invent, are really amazing. Like having four goals instead of two – one on each corner – and being able to score in any one. Or games where you can only score with a header; or with a volley. All these stupid games.

You go out on a Saturday when you've been playing these games, and it destroys you. Drives you mad. Because rhythm is a very important part of your game, but these things screw up your rhythm.

The coaches say you aren't getting enough movement into your game. They say to themselves 'How do I create movement?' Instead of telling players, giving them a direct message, they say 'Well, if we play one-touch they'll have to move, and then after a while, they will be moving automatically.' But it doesn't work like that. If you play one-touch, players will find a way round it. They won't move unless they can see a good purpose for the movement. But coaches try to give these messages to your subconscious, through conditioned games.

Another example is that you might have a team not scoring enough headed goals. So the coach won't say 'We've got to start getting up and winning that ball' and then put someone who can do that into the side. He'll say to himself 'If we play conditioned games all this week, in which you can only score with a header, perhaps they'll get into the habit.'

But of course what invariably happens is that instead of getting into the habit of it, they get so fed up with heading the ball all week that they go deliberately the other way. And the people who didn't like heading the ball in the first place, or were a bit cautious about it, go absolutely the other way. They'll never head it on Saturdays then.

It's the same with one-touch. One-touch games are developed to curb people doing too much on the ball. But if you've got a guy who likes doing a bit on the ball, and you introduce one-touch, he'll hate it. And so, on a Saturday, when he gets hold of that ball, he'll never let it go. He'll do more on it than he ever did before.

So these games can have a counter-productive effect, and it was good that Harry brought matters to a head. But it means that Lawrie's position is being constantly eroded.

13 August

Today we came down to Bournemouth for four days. We always feel very badly done by at Millwall over close-season tours. Orient went to the Bahamas; even Hendon went to Spain; and we come to Bournemouth! But it's always great coming away with the lads, no matter how bad things are at the club, no matter how bad relationships are. And at this time of the year, when everyone is happy and friendly, it's fantastic. Bournemouth seems idyllic – beautiful weather so far, the girls, the sea. And you feel fit and healthy. It's what being a footballer is all about.

It's always the same. You stay at a luxury hotel, and everything is laid on for you. You never have to check in, your meals are all laid on; no worrying about getting a table. You just walk straight in and sit down, and the prawn cocktail is there waiting for you. And you bring your golf clubs, knowing you will be able to play a lot. And there are no responsibilities. For four days there are no bills dropping through your letter box, no wife, no mother-in-law. And no competition, no matches to spoil things. Just the lads.

When every group of footballers go away, it's always the same. And you always have the oddball or the kid; the naive inexperienced lad. And they are always prey for jokes and rags.

Given the limitations of our interests, you could get a bit bored. But you never do. Because the great answer to boredom is finding someone to take the mickey out of. Every club has its mickey-takers, some more outrageous than others. And they are always on the lookout for a victim.

Someone who is naive, or honest. Someone who has a little bit of self-conceit, as we all have, but hasn't yet learnt how to hide it. When you've been in the game a short time, you learn to hide that naive self-conceit. Nothing touches you. But when you first come in, everything touches you. You show your delight, and your emotions.

This trip Gordon Hill looks as if he's ideal for the part. He's very young. He's only been a pro for a couple of months. He's got a lot of ability, but has made no impression on the first team yet. He's just a kid. Coming along because we've only got a small full-time pro staff, and Benny is bringing them all along.

Now the big thing is to be blasé. When you report at the ground in the morning, it's 'Oh Christ, we're not going away again, are we?' But this kid hasn't learnt that yet. He's hopping around from one foot to another chatting away. The same on the coach down. He's really excited. It shows in his eyes. They are all shining, it's all fantastic. He's really chirpy. A lot of teasing and banter, and he's joining in, and answering back. Most kids are quiet at first, but this lad's real chirpy. He's full of self-confidence, thinks he is a very good player, and has seen nothing at the club to make him doubt that judgement.

One thing you never do as a footballer is talk about what you've done. You can kid around in arguments – 'Put your caps on the table, then', that sort of thing. But Gordon made the mistake of telling us what a good tennis player he was, when he heard that tennis would be one of the activities on tour. He said he'd played for Essex in the County Championships, and played at Junior Wimbledon, and been watched by someone from the LTA coaching staff. How they were going to make him another Buster Mottram or whatever. So he really gave us a big opening.

You get bored very quickly, especially in the evenings. As it is pre-season, we've got a 12.00 curfew, which means you can't really go out and get drunk. And we haven't really got any drinkers in the side. So of course the first thing you do is set Gordon up. Kingy is our resident pressman. He's brilliant. So he phones up Gordon in the afternoon.

'Gordon Hill? It's the Bournemouth *Evening Echo*. We'd like to do an interview with you. We believe that not only are you a coming football star, but you're also a brilliant tennis player.'

Gordon had probably never spoken to a pressman in his life before. So this was fantastic. This was confirmation that he had arrived. First he'd been brought on tour, and now here was this pressman phoning him up, wanting to interview him.

'Oh, yes, I am a bit of a tennis player.'

So Kingy carried on the interview, while the rest of us were in there listening. He was superb. He's got a good imagination, and I think after a couple of minutes he had convinced himself he was a journalist. Then he got on to football, and started asking him about the rest of the team, and how long he would take to get a regular place. Now the kid isn't even on the verge, so a modest answer would have been to say that the question wasn't likely to arise yet. But the kid wouldn't say that.

'How long do you think it will be before you get in the first team?'

'Well, it's hard to say at the moment. I've done quite well since I've been here, though.'

'What about Eamon Dunphy? He's a bit of a trouble-maker, isn't he? He must be getting on a bit now too. You could have his place, don't you think?'

'Weeellll, he's twenty-eight. Yeah, I suppose you could say that's getting on a bit.'

'We'll want a photograph, of course. We'll send a photographer round at six o'clock tonight. We'd like one of you in your tennis gear. Have you got any?'

We hadn't brought any with us. But the kid says 'Oh, yes. That'll be no problem.' Of course by now the lads are dying, because on top of everything else, he has now got to hunt around and try to scrounge some tennis clothes. Kingy says 'Right, see you at six' and puts down the phone, and we all disperse.

So Gordon comes rushing round trying to scrounge some tennis gear. And of course Kingy picks him up on it. 'What's all this about?'

'I've got a photographer coming to see me at six. This journalist phoned me for an interview.'

So Kingy says 'I hope you've got the money.'

'What money?'

Kingy turns to the rest of us. 'What do you think, lads?'

'Oh, £25 at least.'

'At least.'

'Oh, but I didn't ask him for any money.'

'Well, make sure you do,' says Kingy, ' 'cos otherwise we'll all have to give interviews for nothing, if you do it. So if you don't ask for it, you're letting the bloody side down.'

Which Gordon agreed to. At six o'clock, Kingy phones him up again, and tells him he can't make it now, he's got stuck in the office, but will be round at nine o'clock. Gordon says yes, that's fine, and makes no mention of the money even when Kingy asks him if everything is all right. Kingy then says 'Oh, there will be a small fee, Gordon. Five pounds. Is that all right?'

There's a very long pause at the other end of the phone, then 'What about ten?'

'Hold on, I'll have to consult my editor.' Kingy looks at us, we have a muffled conversation, and then he goes back and says that is OK, puts the phone down, and wanders off to Gordon's room.

'Did you get the money sorted out?'

'Don't you worry,' says Gordon. 'I told him. £25, or no story.'

Dinner-time came. Kingy waits until Gordon gets his steak in front of him and then nips out to phone him. Poor Gordon had just taken one bite of his steak when it's 'Telephone for Mr Hill.' So he goes out to the lobby, takes the call and then disappears upstairs like a shot. Somehow he has scrounged some tennis kit, so he reappears in five minutes dressed in tennis clothes. We had all agreed to go off to a disco around 9.00, so we're all congregating in the lobby after finishing dinner, and there's Gordon sitting there in white, with a racquet across his knees. Everyone gathers round him; of course we're all stifling laughter, almost choking, but he can't twig the joke.

But he is really worried that we are going to go out without him. And at the same time, he doesn't want to miss the photographer either. We let him sweat it out for quarter of an hour, then Kingy gets on the phone again, and tells Gordon the car has broken down, so he won't be coming this evening. Gordon comes back into the lobby, swearing. Picks up his racquet and disappears upstairs. At which we all went off to the disco. Which was a bit cruel, but he caught up with us there. It was really bugging some of the lads. They kept saying 'How can he be such a mug as to fall for this?'

We had a curfew at twelve o'clock. So when we got back from the disco, everyone was hanging around in the lobby. It was a bit early to go to bed. But there wasn't anything to do. So of course it was 'Let's have some more fun with Gordon.' The question was how? We started off by telling him we didn't believe that he was a tennis player. We thought he was bull-shitting.

'Bullshitting? Bullshitting! I'm telling yer, I played against Warwick-shire in the semi-finals for Essex,' he said. 'Don't worry about that. And I could have gone on the LTA course.'

By now we'd all assumed roles with Gordon. Kingy was his friend and adviser. I was his arch-enemy, really giving him some abuse, telling him we'd heard all this crap before.

'If you're so good,' I said, 'give us a demonstation. Show us your serve.'

'Don't be flaming silly, we're sitting here at twelve o'clock, in the hotel lobby, and you want me to show you . . .'

'Oh, just an imaginary one. You can tell from that. I'll show you my golf swing if you like.'

'Don't be bloody silly.'

But you can see his mind working, and really he wants to give us a demo. All of a sudden he gets up, throws a ball up and goes 'crash'. Of course the lads were going spare; they just couldn't believe it. And there were all these other people around too, ordinary guests. So I said 'Rubbish.'

'You what?' He's really indignant now, and diving in head first. So the next thing is to get him to play an imaginary game in the lobby, with the settees pulled across as the net, against Harry. Harry is club champion at tennis. And at everything else. So we carry on geeing Gordon up, dis-missing his claims, until in the end I can say 'OK then, if you are so good, play Harry.'

'What now? Are you daft?'

'No, only an imaginary game. Harry'll play his shots, and you can show us how you would get them back.'

Finally we persuaded him. So they line up across the settees. 'Thirty-love. Forty-love. Forty-fifteen. Forty-thirty. Out!'

'That wasn't out.' He was really getting in a state now. Protesting violently. Benny and Jack Blackman were there by now, and they couldn't believe their eyes. I couldn't believe mine either. By this time we were wondering just how much more we could get away with before he twigged what was going on. But Benny decided to break it up before it went any further. So we'll have to wait and see.

14 August

We went training at Poole this morning. They are a Southern League team. Semi-professional stuff. Dennis Walker, who was at Manchester United and York with me, has just been appointed their manager. I was really surprised to see him when I walked in the ground this morning. He asked me into the office for a chat. He'd only been there two weeks; and here he was talking about his boys, and how it was different that side of the fence, and all that crap. He'd become a 'manager' in two weeks. Talked just like one, fiddled with his papers and paperweight while he was talking, all the manager mannerisms.

But he came out training with us, and really loved it. Poole are only part-time, so he's there on his own in the mornings, and feeling right out of things. You could see him measuring himself against us, seeing if he was still as fit as he had been. Seeing if he still had it.

He talked about 'them' and 'us'. In his mind he was still a full-timer, still one of us. And yet of course he wasn't really. But it's terrible when you become involved with part-timers. To them it's only a game. To you it's all day and every day of your life.

He made an amazing contrast with Gordon. It really pointed out how your life could change. Gordon Hill had just walked into his life. It was just beginning for him. And then there was Dennis. Someone who had played a few games in United's first team; just been that fraction away from really making it. And now for him it has all ended. And he obviously was really missing the daily involvement. It makes you appreciate how much you get out of the life while it lasts when you see someone who has finished. The same as watching Billy Neill. He was my best mate really. A real, good honest professional. He'd been troubled by knee injuries ever since Palace kicked us off the park the year they got promotion. He finally had to retire last April. Now he's working as assistant coach to Lawrie. And you can see how much he wants to be back playing. It's tragic when you see some who can play and won't, and then see Billy, who was always honest, always wanted to play, and now can't.

Another thing which pointed up our good life was at lunch today. It was really hot. We came in the dining-room in all our casual gear, really happy and relaxed, healthy and fit, feeling just great. And there were all these groups of businessmen in there. Wearing collars and ties and lounge suits and really looking hot and uncomfortable.

There were a couple of middle-aged ones sitting just across from us. I could hear the conversation. They were obviously doing business together. And it was really strained. They were being so polite and formal with one another. Really ill at ease. Lots of 'After you's, and 'Could you pass the salt?'s and 'Would you like a drop more?'s. The kind of conversation I find very difficult to make. And then there was us. Laughing, joking, making a lot of noise, giving the waiter a bad time, and generally behaving very badly in their eyes, I'm sure. But you get into this whole group thing when you are away with the team. You take all your bearings from the group. It's really us against the rest of the world.

The Gordon Hill thing is still going on. Getting more and more absurd. Kingy keeps on phoning him up and putting off the meeting with the most unlikely excuses, and he still hasn't twigged. He went out and bought the paper this afternoon to see if there was anything in.

I'm rooming with Derek Smethurst, which is also providing a lot of amusement to the rest of the lads. It's like computer dating gone wrong. We've got no common interests at all. The thing that sums it up for me is our wardrobe – one of those long built-in jobs. I've got my scruffy gear in one foot, and he's got the other nineteen feet jammed full of his DJs and velvet jackets and what have you.

15 August

A less funny day. Six guys stayed out after the curfew last night. The first came back around two, and the last at four. Lawrie had asked the porter to lock all the doors except the front one, where he sat and waited. When the first two came back they spent about an hour creeping around the back gardens and entrances trying to get in. Lawrie watched them from a window, and finally went out and said 'You might as well come in now, because I've seen you anyhow.'

But what really soured the atmosphere was the fact that one of the guys who stayed out late was Dennis. The club captain, who had just signed a new contract after last week's little set-to. Benny was really upset, he could hardly speak. But he called a meeting this morning. The lads felt bad about it, but again he decided to take no action. He said 'You probably feel ashamed of yourselves', and left it at that. It was a very difficult problem he was confronted with. If he had fined people, or sent them home, he would have created an even worse situation. I would have fined them, I think, but it's a difficult decision. I felt mad about it. I thought it was just totally irresponsible.

We had a practice game against the reserves this morning. Terrible. It was really hot again, and the pitch was awful – full of bumps and holes, and nothing went right. Lawrie was stomping around shouting at everyone, and we were all rowing among ourselves. It's shattering, because we are all convinced this is going to be our season. And when things go as wrong as they did today you begin to get totally frustrated.

The only saver was watching Wolves and Bournemouth in a friendly this evening. Wolves were rubbish. If they play like that, they've got no hopes of going anywhere but Division Two.

Gordon Hill is still waiting for the photographer. He bought the paper again and went through the sports pages at a rate of knots, looking more and more disappointed. He still hasn't twigged. An amazing lad.

16 August

Back from Bournemouth today. The Gordon Hill joke continues. We had him playing imaginary tennis, showing us his strokes, on the coach coming back. Quite amazing how gullible he is. Before we left he was still waiting for that photographer. He just hasn't twigged at all. It hasn't even crossed his mind that he is being put on.

It's probably the longest joke ever. It must seem a bit cruel, but I think the only inexcusable thing was going off to the disco without him. And compared with other clubs, we're quite mild really. Manchester United, when I was there, was wicked. It's all right if it stays within the group. It's when it starts involving outsiders – waiters, or other guests, or the public – that it becomes bad. But within the group it's fair game. The thing is, we're an experienced group, been together for a long time, and there aren't any natural dupes. And the two new lads from Arsenal and Spurs have had it all already, so they are fairly fly. Whereas young Gordon is really green. He'll learn.

17 August

We played QPR in a public practice game at our place today. And won easily. We walked all over them. Frank McLintock was injured, but apart from that they were at full strength. Doesn't look as if I've got to change my opinion about their prospects. I think they will struggle. But it really confirms for us just how good we are.

20 August

I was on a TV programme – *Opinion* – this evening with Danny Blanch-flower and Bernard Joy of the London *Evening Standard*. Talking about footballers' contracts and the retain-and-transfer system. Bernard Joy was representing the establishment, because none of their heavies would allow themselves to be seen debating with a real live footballer. The producer said that Alan Hardaker in particular was very dismissive.

Of course we didn't get anywhere in the discussion. 'The whole basis of the game would be destroyed if players had freedom to come and go as they pleased' etc. And Danny disappointed me by saying that soccer was about risk and adventure, and the security for players which I was advocating would destroy it. But in America baseball and football players have good militant unions, and have even forced the owners to set up pension schemes. It doesn't seem to have turned them into time-servers.

21 August

Everything is geared to Saturday now. Our minds focus on that moment. There is an urgency about our work, we are concentrating on being sharp. Any ache, any heaviness about the legs makes you anxious. It is difficult to measure your fitness this week, and closed-door practice games are about the best guide. We've had two already against Charlton and Gillingham, winning them both comfortably, feeling good, everything clicking into place. Today we went to Chadwell Heath, West Ham's training ground, to play them.

Chadwell Heath is grey and unwelcoming. It was a cold day, shades of

Carlisle in winter. West Ham are talked about as a coming team. Last season they finished seventh in the First Division. Some people expect them to challenge seriously for honours this year.

It should be a good test for us – a mock battle with serious undertones. We weren't going scalp hunting, there was no desire to kick people, but we would be tight, disciplined. After all there were only four days to go.

There was a small group looking on. Mostly reserves and injured players, including Pop Robson and John McDowell. Bobby Moore is conspicuous by his absence. Which provides us with a real talking point. He is the dominant figure at West Ham: captain of the club, and of England. Where is he today? It turns out that he has gone to Crystal Palace Sports Centre to compete in a TV-sponsored pentathlon against Jackie Stewart, Tony Jacklin, Barry John and other leading sportsmen. We are amazed, and yet how typical of West Ham it seems. Here they are four days before the start of the season, their big season, going into a crucial practice game without their leading player. Staggering that he should choose to be absent, crazy that Ron Greenwood should allow it.

It wouldn't happen at many clubs. Certainly not at Leeds or Liverpool. But here it was almost predictable, a confirmation of all the suspicions one had felt about the club.

They have always had talented players. Aristocratic, some say, yet in spite of an occasional flourish on special days, they have never had the commitment necessary to win a League title.

To be sure, they have had some of the aristocrats' qualities: indolence, an unwillingness to sweat, a reluctance to soil their hands.

In a way they were con-men. Like all good con artists they had a certain style. Their play had a smooth, slick quality; it was seductive. Aficionados often purred at the sight of the Hammers, and denounced football for denying the game's prizes to the purists they saw in West Ham.

It was true they had talent, but so did Leeds and Liverpool. They are the real contenders, the true aristocrats. What West Ham lack are values. When the challenge came, their lack of integrity left them at the mercy of the better-prepared, the people who worked at the game.

To Millwall, today's game had meaning. It soon became clear that to West Ham it was a joke. They strolled around, stockings down around their ankles, disdainful. The 'in' thing that afternoon was the curved pass with the outside of the foot. No simple straightforward pass would soil their boots. For a moment I questioned our attitude. Were we taking it too seriously?

Some of their players too seemed inhibited. Patsy Holland, Ted MacDougall, Billy Bonds. Good, honest and talented pros. Bonds played in the back four, because of Moore's absence. I wondered what he thought. Poor Ted MacDougall looked really fed up. He shrugged his shoulders a lot. How could he possibly justify his huge transfer fee among this lot? Of course they would say that he wasn't sophisticated enough for the Hammers. He couldn't do pretty tricks with the ball, or curved passes with the outside of his boot.

We beat them easily, but there was little satisfaction in doing so. Towards the end of the game Lawrie ran alongside the touchline, urging us on. 'Come on, Eamon, son, keep it going, keep going.'

'It's difficult, Lawrie,' I yelled back, 'when you can't stop laughing.'

Afterwards Ron Greenwood stuck his head into the dressing-room. 'All the best for the season, lads,' he said. 'I hope you come up and we stay up.'

I felt he was only half joking. I felt sorry for him.

23 August

I had a long chat with Bryan King last night. We could have problems there. He has done very well, and he knows other clubs are interested in him. He's a big brave lad, a nice lad. A bit of a baby, and a bit egotistical, but then everybody is. He's a real clown, and a good bloke to have in the team.

The trouble is, he's been constantly phoned up by the press, and told that Arsenal or Manchester City or whoever are after him. Of course that makes him want to get away. But the nature of footballers' contracts makes it very difficult to get away if the club wants to keep you. And of course they want to keep him. So he has asked for a move three times now, and been turned down each time.

What happens in this situation is that the player and manager have a very funny relationship. I would think that in the privacy of Benny's office Kingy is a lamb, but he needs to make his gestures in front of the other lads. He's been sulking a bit during training, and he didn't really try in one or two of the practice games. I don't think he's as big a problem as Dennis, because he isn't as strong a character, and I don't think he would ever not try in a real game. But he's been moody when Benny is around. Benny has to tell him to do everything twice. It's a bit worrying, because if you muck around in training, I think it affects your game.

Also I don't think it's in his best interests to do it. He has an interview with Purser and Benny next week, and asked me what I thought he should do. I suggested that his best policy was to get a public commitment from them that if we weren't doing well by Christmas, they would sell him.

He would be a great loss. We have great potential as a group. We have all been together for eight years or so, except Alf, and we feel we have got a lot of good players, we respect each other. We feel that this is going to be our year, over and above the normal feelings that clubs have.

It was different two seasons ago, when we almost got up. We knew we had a good side, but we thought we would need another year or two. It crept up on us, did that season. We made a rare good start – we do not normally start well. The feeling was not as strong as it is now. We have a better side now, a more unified side. We still have factions, but then every club has factions within it. What really matters is what kind of example the senior players set. If the senior players are cliquish and big time, that will affect the set-up right down the line to the apprentices.

In those days, the players with the power were Keith Weller, Dennis Burnett, Derek Possee – and Harry to some extent, although Harry is not really a power figure. Harry goes to work to play only. Those three did not have much respect for Benny, which is ironic because he had taken them from reserve teams, and made them. He gave them an opportunity to become players. But they were self-centred as players. Keith, in particular – he was a good player, but very individualistic, and our most successful period was after he left.

And that year we were a lot more desperate in everything we did. We did get good results, but it was always frantic. We were relying on climbing mountains every week. We would have eighty-nine minutes in our own eighteen-yard box, and then break away and score the winner. While this side is much more capable of going out and attacking.

24 August

Tomorrow the first game. I am confident. Not certain, for that is impossible. The season begins tomorrow and for nine months our lives are committed to the business of winning games.

This is a very special day for football people. Small children lie restless in bed dreaming of the conquests they and their heroes will make tomorrow. Their dads, pints in hand, talk cynically in pubs – 'They will be just as bloody terrible this year.' But in a small corner of their hearts, they too nurture a dream that this will be 'our year'.

More than anyone, the pro dreams tonight. He is more than a dreamer, he is a dream-maker. No matter how long you have been in the game, how cynical you have become, or how terrible you know your team to be, tonight you push the past and present behind to dream of the future, which for you is nine months long.

This year I am confident. There are no certainties, but when I look rationally at Millwall, I cannot see us failing. We have everything. Skill, character, experience, a good crowd. We only need the luck. We should not fail, but we might. If we do, I feel it will be the end for the present side so painstakingly put together by Benny Fenton. It will also be the end of my quest for First Division football.

At twenty-eight, time is not on my side. So tonight I feel a cold chill of fear coming down on my heart. Despite my confidence, I know only too well how fate can cheat.

I believe in what we now have at Millwall. I have watched Benny reshape the club in the seven years he has been there. It was a difficult task, and he has done a good job. Of course I have my reservations, for we are a temperamental lot, Kingy, Dennis, Brownie, and I. Yet I still believe.

2   Early Blows

25 August

Fulham 2   Millwall 0

They had three or four shots at goal, and two of them went in the back of the net. Both goals were breakaways, starting from their own penalty box. Which is ironic, because we used to be defensive and played with a sweeper. We used to do very well out of it. Now we have changed to 4-2-4, which is a very attacking policy. And we had done to us today what we have been doing to other teams for years. When we had Possee and Bridges we used to strike quickly at teams. That happening to us, now that we have gone over to an attacking policy, is sickening.

It makes you wonder whether we should have stayed with 5-3-2. I think it is best to be brave, though. I could not argue that rationally, but I feel it is probably the right thing to do.

For Benny it is a very brave decision. For us it is not so important. If it all goes wrong, we will live to fight on. But for Benny it is his whole career and his whole life at stake. If he gets sacked, I'll be very sad. He has done a lot at Millwall, and he is not recognized for it. He is a very maligned man really.

The older you get as a player, the more you put yourself in the manager's shoes. For a man of his age, in his position, it is an enormously brave thing to do. Three or four years ago I would not have cared about that, but now I feel for him strongly. He must be riddled with insecurity. And he has to preserve his self-confidence whatever happens. If he begins to crack, and we see it, that is the end.

Fulham now will still be in the euphoric state of pre-season training. They will have seen nothing today to cast doubts on their pre-season dreams. In fact they are confirmed, reinforced. Ours are shattered. But the thing about summer dreams is that they are not real anyway. At some stage in the season you are going to come up against the harsh reality. The question is: how valid were the dreams, how near to reality? I think ours are very near to reality. So it is not important that we lost today, except in terms of the two points.

In pre-season training you convince yourself that you are going to be a better player, and you are all going to be a better side. Then as soon as you start playing the first game, the cracks appear. You had thought pre-season that you are not going to miss goals or tackles. But then the first missed tackle, missed goal, and you are back in it all again. The worst goal of the whole season, the worst blow of the whole season, is the first goal. It is like a kick in the guts.

Today they scored five minutes before half-time, when we had been under no pressure at all. We had our chances. Dennis hit the side netting, Gordon Bolland had a header he should possibly have scored with.

Then I gave a pass to Gordon. A bit of a Mickey Mouse pass really. He could have got it, I could have put it nearer to him. One of their defenders lashed it hopefully upfield. It landed at Steve Earle's feet, and the next thing it was in the back of the net. Just before half-time, so we had no time to recover before then.

We walked off at half-time very slowly. It is a great test of character, a situation like that. And Millwall have made some incredible recoveries. In the year we nearly got promotion, we were 3–0 down at Sunderland with a few minutes to go. And we drew 3–3. There is a lot of character in the side.

So at half-time we said 'This is not the end.' We realized that they were there for the picking, that they are not a good side. But they gave us problems because they have this small quick forward line, and we have got big lads in defence who cannot be as quick as them. And we weren't able to recover, in spite of a lot of pressure. They nicked another one.

And that was it. But they will blow up soon.

28 August

The tendency after a defeat is to look for scapegoats. Everybody in the team has doubts about everybody else, but it goes in cycles. There are periods when it is in fashion to not like a particular player's work, or at least aspects of his work. Every player has weaknesses and failings, but some players are easier to get at than others.

When you lose a game, instead of looking for the real causes of the defeat, you tend to take the easy route, which is to say 'He has always been like that, he has always been prone to do that.' The argument following – unspoken – that, as a consequence of him, you lost.

The Fulham game was a classic example of this. I was mad at Brownie (Bryan Brown) all through the weekend. He has got enormous talent, but his attitude is questionable. He is not a bad lad, but being younger than most of us, his problems, which are similar to many pros' problems, are not so well disguised. Most like a moan from time to time. One's own doubts are expressed as criticisms of others. One criticizes the club, the manager, the general situation, but rarely does one look at oneself. To an older pro, the young always seem a touch irresponsible. 'He doesn't apply himself.' In that sense Brownie, in our eyes, pays the penalty for being young.

Now last Saturday, even though I was on the field, I thought the first goal was his fault. I was convinced of this. And I thought the second goal was his fault too. I had visualized that the second goal was the result of a through ball played over his head. The ball was played so slowly, I thought he turned so slowly that he let Barrett in behind him, and the ball was in the back of the net. All weekend I was mad at him, cursing him. We all were probably. He was a convenient scapegoat. But as it turned out, it was not he who had had the ball played past him, but Alan Dorney. My best mate.

We had an inquest today. We went out first and we all practised stopping people taking the ball past us as Barrett had taken the ball past one of the defenders for the first goal. Which was absurd. Twenty-two guys doing the same thing, where there were only two guys involved in the actual game, and ever likely to be involved in it again. But such are the limitations of coaching and some coaches that if one thing goes wrong they immediately set out to put it right by over-compensating.

Players tend to have a fall guy. There used to be a thing a couple of seasons ago when 'Players were not winning the ball in midfield', and I was the fall guy. If we lost 1–0 somewhere, and I had played a blinder and the goal was absolutely nothing to do with me, they would still have a go at me.

The scapegoat thing shows up a lot. It shows how tenuous the relationships are, and how easily they can break down, and how much self-deceit there is in football. You can go on merrily blaming a guy for ages about things which have really nothing to do with him. Teams frequently ignore the real causes of goals and defeats, simply because they are so set in their prejudices.

But there are some players that are never criticized. Even the manager is loath to criticize them, in case they have a go back at him in a really strong way. Benny won't criticize Dennis for one. Dennis is a funny lad. He slides out of games, yet sometimes he dominates the whole thing completely. But he is the captain, and should be a leader. Benny said nothing about him not doing very well at Fulham, because Dennis would stand up for himself. He would deny it, talk back, and Benny would have to argue with him. So rather than have that, he won't criticize Dennis.

A player like Stevie Brown, who is not particularly skilful, *is* open to scapegoating. You get what amounts to a whispering campaign starting about a player. And the longer the whispering campaign goes on, the more convincing the argument becomes. Even to the point of totally ignoring reality. Certainly the current feelings about Brownie do, because he is a good player basically. You don't cut him or anything like that, you aren't nasty to him. It's just that these little whisperings become hard and fast theories, and truths emerge that have no basis in fact at all.

The truth at Fulham was that it was the fault of Alan Dorney, who is one of our best players, consistently so. He was at fault in some way or other for both their goals. But that did not fit in with the theories. 'Alan is a good player. Brownie is a suspect character. Therefore, it must have been Brownie.' And this is incredible self-deception, not only on the part of individuals, but by the group as a whole. This all came out at the inquest, and it took a tremendous effort to take in. I don't think we all realize how often we practise this self-deception.

Crowds do it too. 'So and so is a wanker – is a wanker – is a wanker' and no way, short of scoring a hat-trick each week for six weeks, can he get rid of that.

This is quite apart from all the bollockings that players give one another on the pitch. After a while you hear the mutterings yourself, and then you begin to wonder about yourself.

29 August

Lawrie had us on this stupid routine today, which we all hated. He wanted Kingy working on crosses. But instead of getting Kingy and the two wingers, and working them, he got twenty-four guys, and gave them a ball each. The idea is that you run round the pitch in a circle, taking turns to knock the ball in. The problem is that Kingy is working all the time, but the other twenty-four are only kicking a ball once every four minutes.

Everyone hits the first ball well. But then your concentration goes. You start talking; you're watching the others, and laughing. Then someone will kick your ball away, and soon the whole thing degenerates into a shambles. Because there is nothing in it for us. We only get to hit one ball every three or four minutes. Now if you had a ball between two, you would hit fifty balls in that time, chipping it to one another.

But this guy has the idea that he wants to work the goalkeeper, and keep everybody else involved, so we've all got to do the same thing. Because coaches are afraid to lose control. And Lawrie is afraid that if he just works the two guys, and sends everybody else away to work with a ball, they won't work. So he thinks, 'Well, I'll keep them all here doing the same thing. And let them all get bored together.'

So we did that. You chip one over, Kingy comes out and collects it, and rolls it back to you. Then you go off in a circle, coming back to this point to knock it in again. But on the way round you are chatting, laughing, kicking other people's balls away. There's a stream running alongside the pitch at Peak Frean's, and people were kicking other players' balls into that, or into a clump of nettles. So you had to dive in and recover it before it got carried away downstream, all that nonsense. And by the time you got back to the starting point you've forgotten what you were there for in the first place.

We hate this. But it is a very typical coach's thing. It's what they call a 'functional exercise'. Which sums it up, really. Benny has no time for them. He hates functions. He distrusts them, because he doesn't understand them. And in this case his instinct is right.

A good coach assesses the mood of professionals. He understands their needs. And professionals themselves understand their needs instinctively. You need something specific.

If you've got a winger and a goalkeeper, they both know what they've got to do. And if you are in a routine with someone, a relationship develops and a rhythm comes, and suddenly it's bang, bang, bang. I've often gone out with a ball and a goalkeeper. At first you are just knocking them in, but all of a sudden a rhythm comes. And you are really striking the ball well, and he is collecting well, and it's all movement, rhythm, and good work. It's concentrated. But in a big group thing, interest just evaporates.

While all this was happening, Benny was wandering round, shrugging his shoulders. His dislike of this kind of coaching is thinly disguised. He watches from the sidelines for all the world like a parent indulging a trying child.

Yet every morning Benny, Lawrie and Billy discuss what we are going to do. So presumably Benny was aware of what Lawrie planned for us this morning.

30 August

We had a practice match today, with an awful lot of bickering. Mainly because we were playing the reserves, whose prime object in life is to mess us up. And they do that by not sticking to orthodox positions – you get centre halves tearing down the left wing, that sort of thing. The centre forward will fall back and play deep in midfield, and cock all our midfield plans up. They have got nothing to lose, and they can go mad in these practice games. They know us very well, and what we are trying to achieve. And they will sacrifice their own chances of victory to destroy our chances of getting a coherent strategy together. They really get under the skins of our lads. One or two will mutter 'I'm going to kick that bastard!' out of sheer frustration.

But there is still an awful lot of confidence. One thing which contributed greatly to our recovery from the beating by Fulham was the fact that Palace lost. There is an enormous amount of resentment among players about Palace.

First, because they assumed the Second Division was not much cop, and they would go straight back. That it was really a formality, as to whether they finished first or second in the table.

Secondly, they are resented because they are getting so much money.

Money we are not getting – something like £300 a week if they win. Possee speaks to some of the lads, some of the young lads in particular meet him for a drink, and he is full of Palace and Mal. 'Big Mal' he calls him. 'Big Mal says this' and 'Big Mal says that'; and 'This is going to be "no contest"'. And they all have these tracksuits with their names on them. Or rather these gimmick names. Now I can imagine being in the situation and feeling a fantastic part of it all. It gives you a tremendous 'We are going out to attack the world' approach.

But to people outside of it, it sounds so cheap. It is not so much jealousy as suspicion. In the face of the pro's harsh realities, to hear of some paradise two or three miles down the road makes you suspicious. And angry somehow.

You feel you are only three miles from the Garden of Eden. And when the Garden of Eden loses 4–1 at home it is tremendously reassuring. You can think 'Stuff that! There is no Garden of Eden.'

The fact that they lost 4–1, to what was virtually a Third Division side without its best players, was a tremendous boost, I would imagine, to every player in the Second Division. Not because we fear Palace. I can honestly say that I cannot wait to play them. They have Possee playing in midfield – one of my arch-enemies from the past. I cannot wait to come to grips with him, because I know there is no way he can be any good in midfield. Anyway it was a delight to know that heaven does not exist on earth. Because it certainly does not exist at Millwall.

31 August

When they sign a new player who plays in your position it is not funny. Everyone is delighted they've signed a new player, but you know it is you who is going to be left out, and you are just waiting for it. Stevie Brown was really upset when he heard that Benny had signed this new lad, Brian Clark, yesterday.

Brian was welcomed generally, although one or two of the lads had reservations because he has been around a lot. They feared he might think a move to Millwall was just a gentle kind of change, and another opportunity to get some more money. He is thirty, and so people were a bit worried that he might not have the ambitions that we have got.

Brian is still going to live down in Bournemouth, and come up by train every day, which again is a little bit worrying. You wonder if the commitment is that strong when he does that.

But it was generally seen as a good thing. He is a much respected player in the Second Division. He has been around a lot of clubs: Huddersfield, Bristol City, Bournemouth, and always does a good honest job. Very skilled, good in the air. He is the kind of pro other pros really respect and like.

And it is seen as a good thing because it will solve two problems. Stevie has not been doing much on the right wing, and we only had two in midfield. Clark can go on as extra striker, and a really effective one who can get goals, and it releases Gordon Bolland to come back into midfield. So we are getting a striker and another midfield player.

We have not seen much of him so far. When a player is signed, it is hard to know what sort of a guy he is. I'm sure his signing is a good thing, and he will really be an asset to the team.

The sad thing is Stevie being dropped so early on in the season. In the practice match yesterday none of us were doing all that well, but Stevie was having a particularly bad time. So I said 'Stevie, just knock a few simple balls up, just to get your confidence going.' 'There's nothing wrong with my confidence. I want plenty of the ball. Give it me, give it me!' Remarkable lad.

So Stevie is gone. The lads were a bit cruel about that too. He is a cocky little youngster. Some of the young lads in particular took great delight in mocking him, because he had really lorded it over them. He was 'Flash Stevie' on them. Now he has come down to earth with a bump. Stevie has never been one to adhere to the principle 'Be nice to people on the way up, because you are going to meet them on the way down.'

2 September

Millwall 1   Aston Villa 1

It was very hard yesterday. Things just aren't clicking, although Brian Clark did well, and made the goal.

Gordon Bolland for one is having trouble with his confidence. He has had a couple of great seasons, and he is a really good player. But it is not going right for him at the moment. Balls are slipping off the end of his toe, passes are just getting cut out, and he is missing goals he should score. Again, although he knows it is him, he is looking around for someone to take the blame. When the first defeat occurs, all this starts to happen. The cracks start to appear, and it can be very dicey if the character of the team is at all suspect. Weak teams can disintegrate completely under such circumstances.

But we have never collapsed for that reason. We have managed to pull back from the brink a few times. Yesterday against Villa, we were 1–0 down from pretty early on, and things were looking rocky. They were very physical, and again at half-time we began this thing of looking around for someone to attach the blame to.

Now Benny does not like kicking. It is a strong principle of his. But he said Villa are like bullies in the playground. If you do not stand up and fight back, they will really demolish you. You cannot turn the other cheek in football, particularly in the Second Division. You have got to fight fire with fire. He said that it was no good taking a pride in not kicking people up in the air if people are kicking you up in the air. The only answer was to go out and kick them back. He did not spell it out as clearly as that, but that is what it amounted to.

We are very conscious that we have got character in the side, and these are the times we have got to show it. We went out in the second half with a big job on. We had not looked like scoring in the first half, Villa were very negative, very defensive. It was a big task to overcome our own little differences, and also to simply score a goal and get a point.

We did succeed. We did succeed in pulling back the goal, and we had most of the play. We mixed it physically, and we came out on top in the second half.

Coming off the pitch I said to Trevor Hockey, who had been their main hatchet man, 'How does it feel to be a navvy among artists?'

He just walked on, sneering 'How many caps have you got, then?'

'Twenty-five.'

The crowd were really baying for blood as we came off. There was a really violent, almost evil, atmosphere around the place. Vic Crowe, the Villa manager, was shepherding his players off. When he saw me, he said 'What a terrible place. You deserve £100 a week playing in front of this lot.' I've never believed that terrace violence has anything to do with what happens on the field, but the way Villa played you could see why the fans felt like they did.

The main thing at the moment is that yesterday was a beginning. I think we will go on now and get results, and get better and better. We now have one point from two games, but my confidence is not shaken at all. I think that we are going to be involved throughout the year, and it will be a really good season for us. We have two away games coming up next, then two home games. If we can get six points from that lot, as I hope we will, then we will be well up. And we always get stronger as the year goes on. We will be playing when other teams have stopped.

It is like a marathon race. At the start everyone is bombing. The hares are flying now, but there is a long way to go. Villa will be there, but Fulham won't be. They always stop playing by October. Middlesbrough will be there. It is reassuring that they lost yesterday.

It is very reassuring to look at the League table and see that Sheffield Wednesday, who are a danger, are below us. Hull and Crystal Palace are also below us, and Palace were considered to be a danger, although they are not one really.

We have got over our worst moments, I think. We'll have our setbacks, of course. Probably when we go to Villa. We never do well there. I can't define what it is. It is mystical. We never do well at Craven Cottage either. Fulham always do us there. In the second half we just did not know what they were going to do next. They are that sort of side.

Villa are obviously going to be really defensive away from home. They have a cast-iron defence. They may fail, though. I am not sure that their front runners are good enough to nick goals away from home. They did it against us yesterday, but I don't think they can keep it up through the rest of the season.

The significant thing about yesterday was that in a situation where lesser teams would have been destroyed – 1–0 down against a very good side, in front of our own crowd, having lost away the previous week – we kept fighting. We had enough character and enough faith in one another through years of playing together to keep fighting, although we weren't playing well.

We had tended to look for excuses in the first half. We blamed the referee for stopping the game, and for not giving us this or that, which is a big cop-out really; in situations like that the referee is a very convenient scapegoat.

This often happens with referees. They are not very good on the whole. They are mostly pretty weak, and are mostly lacking in knowledge of how players think. But they do get blamed for things which aren't their fault.

Our problem is that a lot of key players are not playing well. I am not, Dennis is not, nor is Alfie, nor is Gordon. None of us are playing well really, because we are training with a new coach who has changed the coaching techniques. For one thing he has got us standing around a lot. We are not getting enough five-a-sides, and we are not getting any sharp work done, and in consequence we are slipping.

Something interesting happened after the game. Benny came up to me and said 'What do you think?' Benny does not like delegating authority. He has had three or four coaches in the last five years. They were all pretty strong guys. Benny hired them, then did not let them do their job, so they all left. Out of frustration, really. Lawrie is an old Millwall player who played under Benny. He came here after being sacked by Southend. He is not a threat to Benny in the way the others were. He is not more knowledgeable about the game, he is not more popular with the lads. There was a time when all the coaches were more popular than Benny. It would not happen now, because Benny is well-liked. But it used to end up that we liked and respected the coaches much more than we did Benny. And he probably sensed this, and they went.

Now Lawrie has come, and Benny has given him a free hand. The first time he has ever done that.

So when Benny asked me after the game I said 'We are not playing well. I feel sluggish, Dennis feels sluggish. We are not sharp. We are standing around too much in training. His routines are bad. We are not getting enough of the ball, we are not getting enough five-a-sides or sharp tight little situations.'

Which provides Benny with a way back in. So when I said it, you could see the relief spread across his face. He said 'Great. We'll have a chat on Monday. We'll get things together. We will go back to some of the things we used to do: five-a-sides; and sharp sprints.' He said he thought he was not being unfair to Lawrie, that he had given him every chance. That is, five weeks. You could see the relief on his face. He wanted to get back involved in training, which he had not been so far this season. He more or less said to me 'Thanks, Eamon.' Next week he is going to get involved again, and it will be interesting to see Lawrie's reaction.

Lawrie is not weak exactly. It's that he is not knowledgeable. He is an ex-goalkeeper, and goalkeepers know nothing about football. Perhaps this week there will be a confrontation between him and Benny. Benny is going to break it to him that we are going back to the old routines.

Lawrie could be sacked next week. He will be definitely forced into a position where he either swallows his work, and just simply does PT, or resigns. He has only been at the club a few weeks, and his work and theories could be going in the dustbin tomorrow.

Lawrie's big problem is that we all think we know more about the game than he does. I don't mean that to sound arrogant. He is only a couple of years older than me. Dennis, Harry, Gordon and I know the game. We have been in it a long time, we have been pros for a long long time. We have all got fairly good football minds, and we understand a lot of the game tactically. We play in outfield positions, so we know the problems you can be presented with.

Which is not to say that we don't need coaching. It can be a good thing. But Lawrie's way of coaching is to hammer things into you. And coaching, like management, should be about showing people how to express themselves. How to express their own abilities within the framework of the team. Not subjection, but liberation. A lot of coaches see coaching as a way of subjecting people to their particular theories, and this is Lawrie's bag. He is not interested in free expression.

The hard work is good. But you don't need to have a brain or be a good coach to devise hard rigorous training schedules. It is just a matter of pushing people until they are knackered. It is good. You need it sometimes. If he just came out and did the PT and got us warmed up, that would be fine. Getting us fit is one thing. But coaching is something else. Coaching is about influencing players and then a team. A coach should coax people in the same way that a director gets a performance out of an actor.

3 September

You can always pin-point what went wrong when you give away a goal. On Saturday their centre forward nudged Alan Dorney, putting him off balance, and the ball was banged in from about six yards. And so you think 'If I hadn't let him nudge me . . .' and 'It wasn't a good goal – he nudged me!' But if he had not nudged Alan then, probably something else would have happened. But you never recognize that. Football is about self-deception as much as anything else. 'Our goal was a sweet move!' You have blinkers on all the time.

Just how far this self-deception can go is demonstrated by an amazing conversation I had with Chris Lightbown of the *Sunday Times* yesterday. He agreed we have some skilled players, and also that we have character, but he insisted that nevertheless, on the results, we weren't good enough for the First Division. He mentioned a testimonial game when we'd got beaten 6–2 by West Ham, and I kept coming up with all kinds of excuses – like we didn't have Kingy in goal. But it turned out that Kingy had kept goal for nearly all the first half!

So I said 'What about our Cup run? At Everton we had a great result.' And he said 'Everton are a nothing side. You beat Everton, who are a poor side if ever there was one in the First Division, and you lost at Wolves!'

But I *do* believe in this Millwall side, I *do* believe it's capable of getting up into the top three or four. This season will prove me right or wrong. Not only me but Benny and a lot of other people. Most of the other players are very committed, and Benny in particular is committed. It is an unshakeable faith. We have lost our first away game, and drawn at home. But we are not down-hearted.

I don't know what will happen at Blackpool and Preston, but I'm sure that last Saturday's game against Villa will have done a great deal for us. Fulham was a day out at the nut-house. But yesterday was the real war. It was a much more realistic situation, and much more what Second Division football is all about. It was the sort of game that brings you into close touch with the reality of Second Division football, which is graft, graft and graft. And it is character in overcoming situations. 'We shall overcome' is almost the motto of Second Division sides, particularly away from home.

Being 1–0 down against Villa was a hard test of character. It was a test of everything. Of skill and perseverance. The kind of qualities you need away from home, and which we will need at Blackpool. So I think we will get enormous benefit from Saturday's performance.

In the first weeks of the season there is going to be a turning point. Something that can make you or break you. And it can happen in the first six weeks. Most teams will be made or broken in that time. Your dreams will disintegrate, or you will come to terms with reality. Some game is going to spark us off; we are going to overcome some tremendous test. You have to. This is what is so daunting.

If you look rationally at the football season it is a series of hellish tests, Saturday after Saturday. All the Football League is. There are no easy games, no soft touches home or away. You have got a series of mountains to climb, forty-two mountains to climb, in order to get success. Every ninety minutes you play is going to be graft, graft, graft. And at the end of that time the team with the most character, the most resolve, not necessarily the most skill, is going to triumph. Of that I am sure. And I think we are among the top two or three teams for these qualities in the Second Division.

I think Saturday's game against Villa was the acid test. We battered them for that equalizer, they gave nothing away. So that could have been our turning point. If we lose the two away games coming up I would be bitterly disappointed. It would be really shattering, and cast tremendous doubts on what we are about. I think we will get a result at Blackpool. I have fears going there, but more so at Preston. It is like the Villa and Fulham thing. At Blackpool you know what you are going to come up against. And there won't be any 2–0 or 3–0 at Blackpool. But Preston, who knows? They could turn it on under the floodlights. It might be their scene. But we should look to get two points out of those games, three if possible.

4 September

Gordon Hill brought in his tennis certificate and medals to show us today. He's had his kit at Peak Frean's for the last week, waiting to play Harry for the club championship. Harry keeps on putting it off. Quite rightly, because if they ever get on a court, Hill will murder him. So the only way we can keep the joke going is for Harry not to play him.

But we had some fun with the medals. The lads gave him stick. 'Anyone can get a certificate'; 'You probably had them made yourself'; etc. Then I pretended that the writing on the certificate didn't say Gordon but Charlie. 'Go on, they aren't yours, they're your brother Charlie's.'

'Are you blind? Can't you read? Of course it says Gordon!'

So then we started asking him when he was going to put the money for the article into the players' pool, which is non-existent.

'What pool?'

'The players' pool. Everyone puts everything they get from interviews into the pool.'

'Oh, I dunno about that,' he says, and goes to ask Kingy what he should do.

'Well,' says Kingy, 'that's up to you, but they haven't been very nice to you, have they? I'd tell them to stuff it.'

We have been doing this quite amazing function for the last few weeks. It is meant to encourage you to shoot first time as practice for the goal-keeper. But none of us could understand it. I was one of the culprits – could not see it at all. You have the goalkeeper standing between two balls, with two players either side of him. What you have to do, say it was me and Dennis this side, and Harry and Gordon Bolland on the other – I'd chip a ball over Kingy's head to Harry, who would lay it off to Gordon, who hammers it at Kingy. Kingy saves it, throws it out to Dennis, who chips it to Gordon, who lays it off to Harry, who shoots. The idea was to get you to lay things off and to get you shooting first time, and also get in practice for the keeper. But it was all so incredibly complicated, and there was so little margin for error that the thing broke down the whole time. The first wild shot and the ball goes sixty yards for you to go and fetch. And the other four have to stand around while you get it. You get back and have to get it going again. A minute later someone else crashes it, it goes 200 miles in the air, and it has broken down again.

It is a nice idea on paper, but you cannot make it work. You are trying to do too much, you are trying to cover too many points – the goalkeeper, laying up, laying off, shooting. And there is no definition to the thing. No matter how keen you are, it reduces to a joke. So what happens? You start hammering the ball at Kingy's balls, trying to knock him out. It just doesn't work. No matter how keen the lads are, they cannot do it.

To gain anything from your work you have to have something really specific. And you have to be kept fully occupied so that a rhythm develops. Otherwise people end up chatting about what was on telly last night, all that kind of thing. Just the same as in any work situation when things are slack.

62 Only a Game?

6 September

We had a meeting today about referees. The upshot was that we are going to push for the PFA to try and get something done about referees. Alfie and Dennis as the union rep and the club captain were the real instigators. Dennis had been done very badly last week, and nothing was said.

It is one thing that everyone in the game agrees on – the inefficiency of referees. We try and disregard them, really. We talk now in terms of how to get on with the game without them as best you can.

Our feeling, though, is that we work bloody hard all week, we do everything right, deny ourselves a pint, go to bed at the right time, get up on the day of the match feeling edgy, watch what we have for lunch. And you are out on the field for five minutes and it seems that some man can come along and on some whim he just destroys everything you have been working for. You have no respect for the man, you know he doesn't know the game, that he basically is not equipped technically to do the job he is doing. His connection with professional football is rather tenuous. He is there as arbitrator, and you get the feeling that everything you have worked for all week can be destroyed by one of his silly mistakes.

We decided to propose to the PFA that they advocate changes in the system. Either to make the referees they have now full-time, or that ex-players should become referees. I don't think that there is a case for having full-time referees, because it means he is only going to be hanging around most of the time, and he is not really going to learn anything about the game unless he is totally integrated in the way that a professional footballer would be. And as the retiring age is forty-seven, I don't think you can expect a man to devote his career to it. There is no career. But most of the lads seemed to think that was the answer. Benny raised the problem of finances. But everyone said 'Give them £60–£70, give them £100. If you are going to have people, give them good money. When you think there are 20,000 people watching a game, what is £100 here or there?'

7 September

Came up to Blackpool today for tomorrow's match. Dennis and Dougy aren't fit, so we've got Frank Saul and young Gordon Hill with us. Frank is all right. He's a good pro, he does a good job wherever he plays, and he won't let us down. The kid? That is the question.

We had a really useful discussion with Lawrie on the way up here. The situation between him and Benny hasn't been resolved in open conflict. I think Benny must have had a quiet word with him in the office, though, because Lawrie has been very subdued this week.

The discussion was between Lawrie, and Harry, Alan Dorney, Brian Clark and myself. It started off as a general discussion about coaching between Harry and Lawrie; and then I steamed in and made it specific by referring to the row over his five-a-side rules. And after much 'We're not talking about specifics, chaps', we eventually got around to talking about that, which was what Harry wanted to talk about and what Lawrie wanted to talk about.

The gist of what we said to him was that he had good players to work with, players of good character who would do almost anything that was asked of them, and when they did rebel it was time to question the methods. Because it was no small matter for them to rebel. And also that in any confrontation between Lawrie and the players, Benny would come down on the side of the players. And Lawrie acknowledged that.

I think it was a good talk. It was a nice way of saying to Lawrie 'Get off our backs.' And at the same time we were saying to him 'We will do good work anyway, you don't have to be a sergeant-major type to get good work from these people.'

But there are still odd things happening at the club. Like some of the routines we've been doing in training recently. Why does Benny allow Lawrie to put them on? Perhaps because of his reluctance to delegate to his previous coaches, he wants to be seen giving Lawrie a free hand. So that if, as I think is true, he wants to get back into control of coaching, he will be able to do so at popular request.

9 September

Blackpool 1   Millwall 0

We played quite well for three quarters of the game. We were in control, they did not look like scoring, and then bang! They scored. It was in the back of the net.

I made a mistake. I should have closed the guy up. I was knackered. I had been doing a lot of running and again it comes down to character really. I got into a situation where I was very tired physically, which tires you mentally too. It screws your resolve not to make mistakes.

The guy got the ball and came at me, and all I did was make a gesture, the gesture of a tired man. Not only tired physically, but emotionally. He got past me and BANG – back of the net!

Now that goal was my fault. There were other factors involved – other people were in that emotional state too. I should never have been exposed as I was. But what I had done was in making the effort to get there I had gone three quarters of the way that a really good character should go. But I failed in the other quarter of it. Having got there I opted out. So it could be said that I was not the stuff that winners are made of. Or that I am only three quarters of the stuff that winners are made of. But then you could ask questions of other people who never even made the effort.

I knew it was my fault, and the lads knew it was my fault. Curiously the crowd and the journalists never really knew it was my fault at all. They never saw it. Just after the game I was walking out of the ground beside Kingy, and a journalist came up to me and said 'Was your keeper unsighted for the goal?' He obviously did not recognize Kingy, and was implying that the goal was Kingy's fault. So I said 'It was my fault – and by the way, have you met Kingy, he is our goalkeeper?' And the guy tried to disappear into a hole in the ground. Which just shows how limited journalists' knowledge is, how lacking they are. Several people said to me afterwards 'Well done, you're one of the few who played well.' And I had played well in a sense. Yet nobody had seen the mistake, nobody had understood what had happened and why we had lost the game.

After the game I said 'OK, lads, I'm sorry.' And they were very good. 'OK. Don't worry about it, you have worked hard. We all make mistakes.' And I had worked hard. They were very good. We get on well, we like each other to a greater degree than most teams. Socially we have got a good team spirit.

But I was speechless. I could not speak I was so sickened. I really am terribly emotionally involved, particularly this year. And I was disgusted at my own weakness in making that mistake. Ironically too I was beaten because I had not closed the guy up, and when Lawrie had been doing a coaching routine on that the previous week I had said 'I don't need it'. I apologized to him after the game. I could not speak after that.

We went by coach back to Preston to get the 7.40. There is always quite a wait at Preston. We were there nearly an hour. Everyone recovers in their own individual style, and finds comfort with their own group. I sat with Gordon Bolland, Harry and Alan in the buffet and had a drink.

You soon recover in one sense. You have a drink and start laughing. The reaction generally is wry humour rather than despair and blackness. That is what you feel inside. You can always find a scapegoat in those conversations when you are having a pint afterwards. But on this occasion it was impossible for them to mention the real scapegoat, because it was me.

We got on the train and were sitting waiting for dinner. People react in very different ways. Alan as always was very cut up. He takes it very seriously. Brownie was laughing and joking, whistling at the girls going up and down the train. He kept saying 'Come on, let's go and have a few lagers.'

Normally I can recover quite quickly. But I couldn't this time. We were having our meal. Gordon and Alan were a bit subdued and I couldn't get into things at all. I was just gazing out of the window. Normally we play cards. 'Let's get a quick game in before the soup arrives.' But we had no enthusiasm for it at all. I saw Benny sitting with Jack Blackman and the two directors, Purser and Rickard. He was drinking his wine and laughing. I looked at him and thought 'How the hell can you forget it so quickly?' Which is not fair, because it probably hurt him more than anyone. But I was feeling so down because I was the one at fault.

I felt really down all the way back. We always get a lot of supporters travelling with us. They are always in the buffet car. And a lot of the lads will go and have a chat with them. But I couldn't face it this time.

10 September

We were training at Peak Frean's today. Still we have this strange, curiously inert atmosphere. Can't really put my finger on what it is. There's no urgency. Dennis isn't going to be fit for tomorrow. He has an injured toe!

Of course, everyone is very down. But that is all the more reason for urgency. But we were just messing around for the first half hour with Lawrie. No sign of Benny, although he was there.

Then he came out, and we played the reserves, he set up a practice match. I had had a terrible weekend; I had rowed with Sandra, and I was terribly upset.

Anyway, I was feeling really low, and we started this practice match, and Benny was standing there, and he called me over. I had a cold sore on my lip, and he looked at me and said 'Do you feel well?' I said 'Yes, I feel all right.'

And he said 'I'm worried about you. I spent the weekend worrying about you, I even discussed it with my daughter. It's cigarettes, they are killing you.'

I have given up, cut it out practically, and I have never felt better physically. He made me angry. I tried to explain to him that I knew I had made a mistake, but I knew I had not made it because I was not well. I had just made a mistake – no excuses.

And he always says things like this when he is going to drop me. He used to say it in the past – 'Are you well?' And the upshot of it would be 'I'm going to rest you for a couple of weeks.'

I was raging, I was mad, and I could not play – I completely lost control of myself, and I started kicking the ball anywhere. We ended the game, and we had a team talk and a bit of an inquest on Saturday's performance. I was really fuming, and he said something to me, and we had this big row in front of the other players. I said 'Drop me if you want to drop me, but don't say I am sick because I am not.' In a way, it was sad, because you can never tell with Benny how much he is conning you and how much he is genuine.

I think he genuinely likes me as a person and I think he is genuinely concerned at my well-being. But I think he is also the sort of man who would rather drop people who are close to him, in a sticky situation, than enemies of his.

So we were having this row in front of the lads, and the lads started laughing, because I was saying 'I'm well, I'm well! I'm not sick!' And he was saying, 'OK! OK! Calm down, calm down.' They were not laughing at us, they were laughing at the situation. And he said 'Calm down', so I calmed down, and afterwards he called me over, and said 'I'm trying to help you. I'm really concerned about you. You should not say "Drop me, drop me" in front of the lads because I might have to drop one of them, and they'll say "You're dropping me, and he asked to be dropped, and you're not dropping him".'

So anyway he said, 'I'm disappointed in you for that outburst.' So I just said 'You can be disappointed', and I walked off.

11 September

Tonight we play Preston. It's one of those places where anything can happen. We are a much better side than them. And the run can't go on like this. But it's one of those places where strange things can happen.

Benny met me at the station this morning, because I was late. And flustered. And he said 'Calm down, don't get too excited about things. You are a better player when you are calm.' He is always stressing how alike we are. So he also said 'I get emotional too.'

We have this curious relationship. We have rowed and fought more than any two other people at the club, but I think we are basically sympathetic to one another.

12 September

Preston North End 2   Millwall 0

Again we played well for twenty minutes or half an hour. Then the ball came across, BANG in the back of our net. And again it was me. The guy I was marking at the corner scored. I jumped with him but he was better than me in the air. When he scored, my first reaction was to think 'Jesus Christ. I'm cursed.' But it turned out that Kingy was to blame for not coming out for the cross. It was partially my fault again, but the major fault was Kingy's. He should have been off his line quicker. Apportioning of the blame is something which teams do automatically; they see things which people watching do not.

For the rest of the first half I really felt unbelievable. Saturday was bad enough, but now I had gone and done it again. As it turned out, it was Kingy's fault. I could not see it from where I was, but he should have come out and caught the cross. That eased my guilt. But I still felt partially responsible.

Then we went out in the second half and again we put them under a fair amount of pressure. We did not really look good, but we did reasonably well. They got a goal and so it was 2–0. We were beaten again. So now we had got one point out of a possible eight, and yet last night I was relieved. I did not feel like I felt at Blackpool at all. We all felt relieved except Kingy, who sat in the bath for a long time afterwards. He looked terribly downhearted.

It was a relief. We had blown it now. 'That's it. Let's go and have a few drinks.' Which I could not have done at Blackpool.

I had a chat to Alan Kelly and some of the other Preston players. And it made me feel good in a way. You talk to old pros who have been around, and you find that Preston don't think they are going to have a good year. It is going to be the same old struggle for them, they think. Alan Kelly said 'This three up and three down, we are worried about the three down part of it!' Their reaction to the change was 'Oh no. It's going to be harder to stay up,' whereas our reaction had been 'It gives us a better chance to get into the First Division.' That is the difference really. That is why we will finish above Preston.

You feel relief because it takes the pressure off. I was relieved. I went out and had a drink. I thought 'Think about other things. Think about what you can do in radio, journalism, coaching. Your sort of second strings. Think about making money instead of achieving something. Think about compensations.' Which is all money and punditry can be. Football is my real work, and anything else is really a poor compensation. My thing this year has been to do something with football. To get promotion. The Preston game seemed to say to us 'No way. No way.' The same old story. And being an old pro, and particularly after speaking to other older pros at Preston, people like Alan Kelly, Alan Spavin, who have been around and never really achieved anything although they are distinguished professionals, is comforting somehow. It is a relief, and it is a tempting situation to accept.

Kingy recovered in a way that I probably could not. I don't know. Alan Dorney would not come out with us. He went to bed. He would have come out if we had got a result. He takes things very much to heart. He said to me today 'You wake up in the morning and you think "One point". The first thing you think of is one point.' He cannot shrug it off, and I can't either. The first thing he thinks about when he wakes up! That is the difference between people who love the game and are com-

mitted to their work, and have a sense of responsibility, and those who
don't and aren't and haven't. It is the difference between teams who do
well and teams who do not. And that is why people who rave on about
West Ham annoy me. Because those guys have more talent than us, but
they have not got the character, the commitment.

Our despair is probably the same as that of the kids who follow Millwall
and wake up like Alan thinking 'One point'. It affects them very deeply.
At Millwall we have got more players like that than other clubs have –
there cannot be many clubs with more characters than Kingy, Kitch,
Harry, Alf Wood, Alan. Men who really hate to lose and who would really
die to win again. We have got a lot of ability in the side too. It has not
come through in these early games, but we have.

And the combination of character and ability and good players is
enough. Or should be. But it is very complex in football. You can have
all of those things and have bad tactics, weak leadership, just bad luck,
which we had at Blackpool, and you have had it. To be successful you
need so many things.

We have got the hardest things to get – the players, the character, the
skill. And that is why it is so hurtful. The other things you can get. Good
tactics are not the hardest thing to devise. Luck you cannot devise, it is
in the lap of the gods. But you can get good organization; good leadership
you can get.

These last few weeks we have certainly been badly organized tactically.
We have lost, I would say, two or even three games through bad tactics.
Benny made a decision at Blackpool, after twenty minutes, to pull Frank
Saul out of midfield to mark Suddick. It left us short in midfield, and I
think that cost us the game. I said that to him, and he said 'OK, what
would have happened if I had left things the way they were? Suddick
was creating havoc. I could see him scoring any minute. We would still
have been one down, and as it was we nearly did it, and it was a stupid
mistake on your part . . .' Which is right.

So he has got to balance these things up. We did not go up to Preston
for one point. We went there to go out and play as best we could. We had
three strikers. We weren't playing well. We have so many players who
are not having it off. It was not that we were playing defensively, but that
we kept giving the ball away to them, who attacked us. So we were under
pressure all the time. Which is different from playing defensively. We

have not played defensively this year. We have simply been playing so
badly we have kept on giving the ball away, so we are always under
pressure.

We are just having a bad time. We have got good players playing badly.
Alf. Every game for him has been a nightmare. I think football is founded
on people like Alf Wood. Guts, guts, guts. He would run through a brick
wall, he would die if he had to. He is having a bad time. Gordon Bolland,
a beautiful player when he is playing well, has lost his confidence. He
cannot do a thing right. This trouble he is having can just arise from
anything. He had a good season last year. Then something clicks in your
mind, you have a bad game, or something worries you, and all of a sudden
the ball you trapped automatically last year you are having to think about.
And it is not coming off this year. Confidence is a fragile and delicate
commodity, and you cannot answer the 'Whys?'. If you could, you could
turn ninety per cent of the players in the English League into better
players overnight.

The only thing you can say with certainty about lack of confidence is
that it comes to every player and to every team at a certain time. We
played much of last year on top of the world, knocking the ball about
beautifully. We cannot do it now. So what do you do when you lose
confidence? Leeds have won their last seven games – I guarantee that
before Christmas they will lose two games or have a similar crisis. They
will certainly draw at home; which for them is a crisis. But they will
react positively and get over it. Because they will work at it, they will
work harder, they will fight harder to overcome it. They will want to
overcome it. They won't cop out. Whereas West Ham, who are having a
crisis now, won't react well to it. Fellows in their side who are lacking in
confidence will hide.

Fellows in our side will even try and get in the game more. The more
mistakes Alf makes the more he wants the ball. And the worse he looks.
Rather that than that he went away and hid. This is one of the crucial
things that makes great sides. Which you never see mentioned in the
press. But that is what it is about: people being willing to make mistakes
when they know how bad they look. They keep wanting the ball at times
when every time you get the ball at your feet it is a personal crisis.

That is the stuff men, heroes, are made of. That is what football is all
about. It is certainly what it is all about in the lower divisions. It is what

sport is all about. Seeing a challenge and accepting it. And accepting the risk of failure.

The Second Division is full of guys who have not got the right technically to be there. Some have not got the right to be earning their living out of football. But they have got guts. At school they were not the stuff that champions are made of, football stars are made of. That was what the gods said, that is what their ability said, that is what their sports master said.

But *they* said 'I'm going to work at it, I'm going to put myself up for ridicule and make mistakes. And I'm going to fight, fight and fight.'

One of the great things about being a footballer is the away trips. Not so much the playing, but the travelling away, the card-schools and the stories, and the joking. That is as good as getting a result. It is great when you get a result away from home. But one of the reasons it is great is that then you can enjoy the other things aside from the game so much more. The manager probably lets you stay out later, you go to a nightclub and you feel great. Really happy with the world.

If you get stuffed you still go out, but it is not the same. You have a few beers and talk about other things, but sooner or later you come back to the game. It's 'What about this, or that?' Or 'What about that goal?' And the manager tends to want you in at midnight, as opposed to three o'clock.

We got stuffed and things look grim at the moment. But the journey back was still enjoyable. There is this comradeship which is expressed through the card games and the leg-pulling.

At Millwall we don't play for very high stakes. At some clubs there is a lot of heavy gambling, which I think is wrong, because people get upset. I've seen lads lose £20 on the way to a match. That can't be right, because you are sick before you get to the ground. It doesn't necessarily affect your performance, but it might. And it is no good anyway, because it means you are taking money from your mates.

Harry, though, really likes a bet, and so do I. One night we were sitting in a hotel, bored, and there was some golf on TV. So he and I were betting on the putts. Waiting until the player got onto the green, then having even-money bets on whether the putts would go down. He would bet on anything.

He is a great character anyway. In many ways the life and soul of the club. In one sense he is a butt for everybody. Not because he is a fool, but because he is such a shrewdie. And a comical character. Jolly and heavy and a bit cumbersome. But he is very shrewd. When I first joined Millwall I suppose he thought I was a green young lad from the North, which I probably was. He met me in the car park one day when I was going through my LP phase. And he had a load of LPs tucked under his arm as he was getting out of his car.

'Morning, Eam,' he said. 'Here, you like LPs, don't you? Have a look at this lot.' And they were by someone I liked at the time – I can't remember who. 'Look, let you have it for a nicker.' What a bargain! So I gave him the £1 and got the record. But I was going back up to Manchester that weekend, and as I was standing at the station bookstall browsing through the books and records, I spotted it among them. For 12s. 6d. So I thought 'You swine, Harry.' But the thing about him is that you can't dislike him. He is the lovable con-man. That is his thing.

He is one of the card-school we have on trips. Everyone has his own thing. Lawrie does crosswords. Then there is the *Penthouse* and *Playboy* gang. Dennis always brings a lot with him, but they usually get devoured on the way up. We had a chess craze for a time. Alan and Dennis had this little pocket chessboard which they brought away and that screwed up the card-school for a time.

When we all finish the game the great thing we will all remember won't be so much what we won or lost as the trips we had and the fun.

Even at international level that is true. I got twenty-five caps, which is great really, but what was great about it was the people and the trips. The fun we had in Paris or Prague or wherever, and the little jokes we played. When you are not involved, those are the things you miss. Because most of the time the actual playing tears your guts out. It worries you, frets you. Even the honour of it, which is something very profound, never really hits you at the time. To stand there, when you play for your country, hearing the National Anthem, with your parents and relations and friends in the stand, is the greatest thing in your life. But it is greater for them, because they are watching and enjoying it. At the time you never really feel as if it is happening to you. You enjoy the day before and the day after more.

I saw Shay Brennan in Ireland during the summer, and he told me about his and John Giles's first trip abroad together with Ireland. They were rooming together. And Gilesy is noted for how much he loves his sleep. Shay had to get back to Manchester quickly after the game for some reason. So he had to catch a very early flight the morning after the game. He had to leave the hotel at around 6 a.m. He was leaving with a couple of the selectors, who also had to get back for business reasons.

So he was creeping around making sure that he didn't disturb John. He crept out, got downstairs and went into the street. He looked up and there was John standing at the window waving good-bye to him.

Shay said he thought 'What a great bloke. He loves his sleep so much, yet he has got up out of bed at this hour to wave to me. Fantastic.'

It turned out though that John had lain awake when Shay was getting up, and had decided, as the final joke in a series they had been playing on one another, to tip a bucket of water over Shay as he came out of the hotel. But when Shay came out he was with the two selectors. So John had had to leave the bucket of water by his feet. And when Shay looked up, he had waved.

That must have happened ten or twelve years ago now. But Shay still remembers it. It is one of the fantastic memories he has got of the time when he played. He can remember that better than he can listening to the National Anthem before the game.

13 September

We pulled another beauty on Gordon Hill today. I got this photographer mate of mine to come down, pretending to be from *Goal*, to get pictures of Millwall's new 'star'. It was incredible; Dave had him standing on his head, pulling funny faces, the whole bit. Then we pretended to want to get in on the act. Everyone was saying 'How about one with me, Gordon?' Of course he chose Kingy. 'Don't take any notice of Dunphy,' Kingy told him. 'He's just jealous because he's old, and no one comes to take photos of him any more.'

'You watch him, Gordon,' I said. 'Kingy'll put the knife in your back sooner or later.'

'No,' said Gordon, 'he's my friend. He wouldn't do that.'

Poor Gordon. He's a bit like Best was at Old Trafford. In another world most of the time, not really part of the group, completely detached from reality. But George was never that gullible.

The final coup was throwing a bucket of water over him. Dave played it beautifully. 'Oh, I missed that. Could you do it again?' So we left Gordon soaking for several minutes then repeated the performance for Dave to photograph it.

14 September

Overall there has been a very strange mood at the club. An acquiescence somehow. The Dennis thing is strange. He is a key player and he has got a bruised toe. Tomorrow he will have missed three games with that bruised toe. There is a curious acceptance of it by Benny. Whereas normally he pushes a player to get fit and may even play him if he is not completely fit, he has not pushed Dennis. At least not overtly. And Dennis has not seemed particularly keen to get fit. Maybe I am misjudging the situation, but it seems part of the general atmosphere this week that there has been a lack of dynamic activity. Everyone is curiously flat.

It may have been relief. When you have a situation like ours, not winning any of our first four games, there is a kind of relief that the pressure is off somewhat. Your fate is sealed. You feel that things are not going to work out, and people tend to accept it and say 'Ah well, that takes some pressure off, and if we don't win, well, we don't win and what the hell?'

In that kind of situation you need a good leader, a good manager to come out and rekindle the flame. You need someone to keep you going, because it is tempting to slip back into the old acceptance of mid-way results. That is what most teams do at this time of year. You go hard for the first month, and you are still in your dreams, and you can see a possibility for success. But the problem with that is that it puts you under pressure, because it makes every game vital. It makes everything you do vital. It is really nice to be in a position where you can achieve something. But it has its pressures. And then there is the old thing of being afraid of success.

Lots of sportsmen are afraid of success because they cannot cope with the pressures it brings. They do not welcome it. At the first sign of failure they accept it with almost a sense of relief. They are going to settle down to mediocrity, there are going to be no pressures and they can indulge themselves.

And this is the difference between teams that achieve something, great teams, and teams that do not. It is the difference between players that achieve things and players who do not; managers who achieve things and managers who do not. At some stage in the season, failure is going to stare you in the face. Even with a team like Arsenal when they did the double. At some stage that year they lost 5–0 away from home.

It is the way you react to defeat, or to the signs of failure when they come, that determines everything. What Arsenal did was to come to grips with that defeat. They reasserted their desire to succeed; they went out and did not lose a game for about the next ten. They did not succumb to the temptation of opting out.

3 Peaks and Valleys

16 September

Millwall 3 Hull 0

The way we are playing, we do not deserve to be challenging for anything. But we are not going to stop. We are not going to go the way of others. And yesterday again, we came out and played terribly. But we fought on. We plugged on and we got a result.

We've always felt we have a lot of character in the side. Which in football terms means the ability to go out and be positive when things are going wrong. To try and reverse what seems to be your fate as opposed to accepting it. Before yesterday we had one point out of a possible eight. A terrible situation. There are two types of footballers. Those who will drop their heads on their chests when things are going wrong, and those who will say 'I'm going to get on top of it. Work harder and be positive.' We've always had more of the guys who wanted to be positive. In our side it is difficult to jack it in because there would always be someone at your elbow, shouting in your ear 'Get your head up. Let's keep going.' Harry in particular is great at that.

Before yesterday's game Harry was walking round the dressing-room with his fist clenched. 'Come on, now, let's have a go. Let's have a go! This is when we need each other, when we're struggling. Let's have a go!'

It's a bit of a gee, a little bit of psychology before you go out. You really need someone in the dressing-room who is prepared to stand up and do it. It's very important. The dressing-room is where you build up your resolve before the game. Especially the last half hour beforehand. I've heard managers say that you can tell whether a team is going to do well or not from the atmosphere beforehand. Doing well in the lower divisions is as much a matter of resolve and determination, of attitude, as any other factor. You can sense in the last ten minutes what is coming. People are talking to one another, wishing one another luck, getting generally psyched up for it. On a wet cold day, like yesterday, you don't fancy it really. If you were rational, you would much rather be sitting at home in front of the box. But this is what makes people professional footballers. You have to go out in the cold and the rain and do it.

And what makes that happen is what goes on in the dressing-room before the game. It would have been easy in our situation not to fancy it yesterday. It was a terrible windy afternoon. Bleak English September. The crowd was down to around 6,000. They were sick with us already; just waiting to have a go. The pitch is like trying to play marbles on cobblestones. So if there are any doubts, any flaws, they are going to come out. There's going to be no joy out there. You are going to go out of the dressing-room door knowing that for ninety minutes it is going to be hard. They have probably come to kick, the pitch is bad, and the crowd are just waiting for a scapegoat. Every time you get the ball you know you're a target. The only thing which can get you out is a good atmosphere in the dressing-room. A good gee-up. The feeling that you're all together. Someone simply saying 'We think we are something. Let's go out and prove it.' Something to take your mind off the reality of our position. When you are struggling as we are, that is essential.

Benny isn't a Bill Shankly. Some managers can send you out on to the pitch willing to die for your country. But Benny is a quieter operator. He gets individuals on their own. Once he said to me before our key promotion game at Norwich 'You're an international footballer. You're different class to these. Now go out there and prove me right.' I'd been having a bad run, but I had a great game that day because he had turned a key in my mind. That's his thing. But he isn't a great one for sitting us down collectively and setting the group on fire.

But Harry is. He was great yesterday. We couldn't wait to get out when he had finished. We were almost ready to tear the door down to get out there. His attitude, his enthusiasm shines through, and it rubs off on everybody else. You think 'If he can do it, I can do it. We're in this together.' If you don't have that, you don't have a team at any level in this game.

And this is what we are good at, this is what we have done time and time again. Other teams stop playing by October; but we will be going on through the winter, overcoming adversity after adversity, overcoming bad performances. We will plod on, we will grind our way up that table, and we will get into a challenging position.

Gordon Hill played his first home game yesterday. He had played at Blackpool and Preston. It is amazing to think that he has only been at the club a few months and is already in the first team. He is not ready yet. He needs to spend a lot longer in the reserves learning the game. You just never know what he is going to do, which makes him impossible to play with. And he gives the ball away too much. The crowd have taken to him in a big way. There is nothing like a few tricks on the ball to get a crowd going, even if the tricks don't get you anywhere and just put the rest of the team in trouble. Dougy should be fit soon enough.

Alfie still is not playing well either, which does not help. But he is trying harder and harder. Benny had a go at him for some reason at half-time. They had a little row, but it was nothing much.

We have got one big problem in that we miss Gordon up front, we are a bit sluggish now. Alf and Brian Clark are similar types, and we lack that incisive thing we had when Possee was there, with Gordon. And we miss that very much. But when Dennis comes back into midfield, it will release Gordon to go up front.

It is amazing, though, the way things change. The Second Division table will be very different in a couple of months. I think Villa will come out on top inevitably. Middlesbrough too. Character and ability. And we will get up there, I know. We were bottom before yesterday. We are fifth from bottom now, but we will get our way into the top six.

I think that with this result behind us we will go on to get results away from home. We will beat Sheffield tomorrow. We might have a little run now – go five or six games without defeat, haul ourselves into fourth or fifth place and hopefully be up there all year.

Dennis worries me, though. If he is cynical, which I think is possible – I don't know – then he may be thinking he is all right. Because then people he is in with, some of the directors, could take over if things go on being bad. A coup by the directors – I could see that happening. And if it does it could put a major obstacle in the way of us doing well. And then I would opt out. Because I cannot be half in something. It has to be all or nothing.

The thing is, Dennis and Benny have never got on. It is quite amazing

the bad relationship between the captain and manager. Dennis is con-
temptuous of Benny, and Benny has been weak and suffered Dennis, even
though he dislikes him. I hoped that it had all been sorted out at the
beginning of the season with Dennis signing a new contract. But it has not.
There has not been open war as there was in the past, but they don't
really communicate.

At times in the past Benny would turn on Dennis and tell him what he
really thought of him in a temper. And then next match he would still
give him the ball to lead us out. It has always amazed us. There was one
crisis meeting last season when Dennis said something. Benny turned on
him. 'Listen, you bastard. You never train, you've never done a job for
me on the field; you've done nothing but moan, moan, moan and go to
the boxing with the directors. And you're supposed to be captain of this
side.' But in spite of all their confrontations about training, tactics, and
everything else, Benny respects strength to a ridiculous degree.

I've got on much better with Dennis recently. I'm going to play golf
with him on Tuesday morning. We never used to get on, until we started
playing together in midfield. Then at Sunderland he caused a goal to be
given away. Everyone is very reluctant to have a go at Dennis. But I
slated him on the pitch. I said it all right to his face. He went spare, and
never tried a leg for the rest of the game. But he respected me, and I think
still does, because he knows I will tell him straight. He is a funny character, Dennis. He is not a bad lad in himself, but I suspect he is cynical. And
his relationship with the directors is bad.

It undermines Benny. Benny is all right as long as Purser stays as
chairman. But I think some of the directors would be delighted to get
Purser out. And if he went Benny would be gone too.

I would hate to see Benny exposed to that. I think that overall he is not
a bad man at all. He has got his faults, but so has every manager. He has
had a hard life in football as a manager. He has been sacked a couple of
times. He is fifty now. If he were sacked from Millwall he would have
nothing.

We have got failings, but I still think we are on the brink of something
that Benny has tried to create over the years. He has tried to sign good
people for the club, nice lads. If he went I think power would go to
Purser's enemies. And that could mean a different type of club. The values
would be different. We would end up losing the emphasis on character

and on genuine people like Alan Dorney. The flash cars, money, boxing and dinner-jacket set would take over.

We had some of that when we were doing well. A few of the players would tell us 'how they were doing it'. The rest of us were there to do the spadework. They saw success in football as a chance to flaunt that success in other people's faces. What it meant to them was that they were in-trinsically better people than anyone else. Their values were better values; their cheap, shallow way of life was better. Their Anglo-American boxing, their big cars, their sunshine holidays were what success was for.

And it led to young lads being abused in the club, persecuted in little ways. It led to divisions within the club between players. Every year some-body would do well; he would then become part of the 'big scene'. He would take liberties in training, come in late for training, probably get more money. Some players got more money than the rest of us and they used to come into the tea-room every Thursday waving their wages slip. Laughing and joking, saying 'I'm getting £30 or £40 more than the rest of you.' That kind of thing is bad. It is bad for the club, it is bad for other players. It is not bad that they are getting more money – Kingy and Dennis both get more now. But they don't come in like that and shout about it.

We have got good people now. This is the make or break year for us. I think we can make something of it. It would make some sense of my footballing life if we got promoted this year. It would give it point that it would not have if we fail again. I think Benny has built nearly a good thing, given the limitations that are on him.

18 September (see also pp. 170–76)

Millwall 1   Sheffield Wednesday 0

We're on our way. Only four points behind the top side now, two wins in a row setting us up. And this one was a good win. We're still not playing really well, but last night's was a great result. They are a good side, but we expected to beat them.

For the first twenty minutes they played us off the park. We played reasonably well, but they were the better side. But we worked at it; had a couple of chances, which we missed. In the second half we went out and there was nothing. Nothing at all in the second half. Then slowly, as we kept plugging on, plugging away, we got on top. They didn't really want to know. But we weren't really good enough to capitalize on it. Then in the last few minutes we put the pressure on. I got a free kick into the box and Alfie headed home, one minute from time. Fantastic.

We were all ecstatic. Everyone was singing, Benny was beaming, delighted. Then I went upstairs to the players' tea-room to meet some friends. And one said he thought we were lucky. Not true. We showed more character. We kept going for ninety minutes. We kept plugging on, we kept wanting to win.

So at last it's coming together. We're no longer stranded with one point. Four points from the last two games. It's coming right. And Dennis surely must be fit for Saturday. Having him back will be a great asset.

The thing about last night's game was that it was in many ways a game we should not have won. In terms of football we were outplayed. They have a lot of skilful players – Craig, Rodrigues, Sunley, Knighton, Potts. And in the first half they played very well. They had a couple of chances they did not take.

We were not playing well. But the thing in a situation like that is: are you going to get a result, or is the obvious going to happen? Can you cheat fate and nick something which you are not entitled to?

What happens to middle-of-the-table sides, or sides that just fail, is that when they don't deserve to get anything, they never do get anything. They go away from home, are under pressure for ninety minutes, and lose 1–0. Whereas a side that is going to achieve something will go away, be under pressure for ninety minutes, not play very well, and still get a 0–0 draw, or nick a goal in the last minute and win 1–0. That is what it is about. That is crucial. Because all the time it is not going well it is a test of character. A test of how much depth and substance there is to your character as a side and as individuals. To be a challenging side, you have got to get 0–0 draws.

Even at home, when you play badly, you have got to be able to get some sort of result. As opposed to caving in and getting done.

Last night we were in a situation which put us to the test. We were not playing well; we didn't deserve anything. If it is going to be your year, it is the kind of game where you have got to get something. You have got to beat them.

And in the second half we demolished them. We piled on the pressure, we got in very quickly, and completely turned round the flow of the game. We got on top. The only question was whether we would be good enough to nick something.

So it became a different question. We had answered the first question, which was 'Could we fight our way back into it, despite the fact that things had not been going well?' We had done. Now the question was being asked of them – had they got enough character to cheat fate and nick a result, when it looked in the second half as if they weren't going to get one?

That is the fundamental question in football. It tells you a lot about how the year is going to go for you. This kind of game is much more important than the kind you win 3–0. Against Hull it was over twenty minutes from the end. We weren't asked serious questions about our character. Games like that, in the sum of a season, mean nothing. You are going to have them whether you are a good side or a bad one. You are going to get results cheaply. But what sorts out the good sides is that they get results when it is bloody hard.

We were able not only to get back on top, but to have enough character, enough desire, to still want to win. It was a battle. We got to two minutes from the end. They looked OK. They had every reason to think they were OK. We got a free kick which I knocked into the box. It was a keeper's ball, and he never left his line. So Alfie nipped in, and bang! Goal! GOAL!

Now that was significant. It tells you a lot about Sheffield Wednesday. There they were, done really well, two minutes from the end, and they still had not got enough character to make the effort to get off the line to get the ball. They were in position *A*, and they still couldn't find enough. So what are they going to be like if they were 2–0 down away from home? No way are they ever going to come back. And that is what you have to do. The year we just missed promotion we were at Sunderland 3–1 down with two minutes to go. And we drew 3–3. That is tremendous, at Sunderland especially. To get out of a situation like that and get a result you have to have a special quality: character, belief, desire.

You can break up a successful team's results in football. Fifty per cent of the time you play really well, you are the better side on the day, and you get what you deserve. Twenty-five per cent of the time you are in very tight situations, very close games, and you get what you fight for, what you claw your way up to. And twenty-five per cent of the time you get a terrible chasing, and you still get a result. You have kicked it off the line. Someone put his head in where the boots are flying, and cleared off the line. Someone has made a last desperate tackle. The full back has come across and covered the centre half, where he has no right to be, and cleared it.

The reason you get those results is that you have got a full back who is keen enough and honest enough to not simply be satisfied that he hasn't given any goals away, but to feel responsible for the mistakes others make. In a situation like that the opposition aren't playing eleven players; they are playing twenty-two. Because every one of your players feels responsible for things over and above his own job. So he is doing two people's jobs. So you have got fifteen, sixteen or twenty-two people on the field in a very real sense.

That is not just a cliché. You really have. Your back four is really a back eight. Because if the full back makes a mistake, one of the others wants to help him. That is why in a bad side you hear the expression 'I thought they had sixteen players on the field.' They did. And the bad side might have two or three cowards in their side, who don't want to play. So they have only had six players.

And that is what has been great about Millwall over the years. We have always had sixteen or seventeen players on the field. Take Alan Dorney. He blots his man out of the game. And perhaps Brownie is having a bad time. The winger slips him, cuts in for a shot, and who appears? Alan. Bang. He blocks it. So you have got two right backs. And that is duplicated right through the team.

In the Second Division ability has levelled out. Most sides in the Second Division have got about the same side on paper. Two or three very good players, five or six good players, add a couple who aren't quite there. And that is what it is all the way through. So in the end it comes down to organization, and to who is going to make the effort. That is why this result against Wednesday was so great.

People can sit in the stand and say 'They were better, they were more aesthetically pleasing. They are doing what the game is all about.' But they aren't. They are doing *part* of it. But the game is about competition, about conflict, about character. Certainly at our level. So what we did was great last night. We achieved what was crucial, and what will stand us in good stead over the season. You can go and beat someone 6–0 and what have you proved? That they are a bad side. Not necessarily that you are a good side. But after a game like last night you come off feeling really proud. You think 'Great. What a good set of lads. What a great result.'

You feel secure. You think 'Well, whatever happens next week, it is not going to be any harder than that.' Once you have done it, you can reproduce it. You have proved that you can kill yourself in a game, really punish yourself. It is the 0–0 and 1–0 results that make the difference, not the 3–0s and 5–1s.

People were raving afterwards about Tommy Craig. I've played against him several times. He has great skill, and he is strong. If he wanted to play, if he had the desire and application and courage to go out there and play for ninety minutes, he would be a hell of a player. But he doesn't. He never plays well the whole ninety minutes, even when they do well, against us. They don't often do well against us anyway. And part of the reason is that although he is a better player than I am, or Frankie, he won't keep going. He gives me a chasing. First twenty minutes he is knocking the ball past me like nobody's business. And then all of a sudden I'm still running and he has stopped. And in the last half hour I'm getting on the ball and doing more. And probably over the ninety minutes I do more than he does. I do more running. I do more off the ball, because when we are attacking, he is non-existent.

Which tells you a lot about Sheffield Wednesday. If I tried to play like him, to concentrate on doing it on the ball, and using my skill to the exclusion of chasing and rushing about, I would never be in the side. The clubs I've played for won't stand for it. At Millwall if you don't put the graft in, you won't be in the side. And we always finish higher than they do, we have come nearer to doing things than they have. And that is the reason.

I could probably play for Wednesday, and everyone would say 'What a lovely player. Doesn't he do well.' And they would accept me poncing around.

But sooner or later they will get a manager who is going to achieve something. And he will say 'Look, Tommy, this just is not good enough. You have got to work!'

And the other thing is that when he starts grafting and working for ninety minutes, he won't be able to do as much on the ball. Because he will be knackered when he gets it for a start. He will have spent two or three minutes trying to get it. And that determines what you can do on the ball.

If you are a midfield player there are two sides to the game. One is getting the ball and playing when you are on it; the other is getting it back when they have it. And the more you do to get it back, the less you are able to do when they have got it. And the less good positions you are going to be able to take. You might not be able to get on it as often as you would wish. Take Johnny Haynes. They used to say 'What a great player he is at finding space.' The reason he was able to find space was that when his opposite number had the ball, Haynes was nowhere near him. He was thirty yards away, waiting for the attack to break down so that he could have the ball. Of course he found space. But he didn't have to get back to deny other people space.

It's a question of what you have to do to stay in the game. I've found over the years that, although I've got a lot of skill and could be a very skilful player, I've never been allowed to indulge myself. I've always had to graft to get the ball back, to shut people down, to close it up, to make it tight for the opposition.

I had a choice to make a few years ago, and I chose to be that kind of player. A bit of a rusher around, rather than a cool 'put your foot on it' man. By Millwall standards perhaps I've still been a 'put your foot on it' man, but for me the game now is ninety per cent effort, and ten per cent do it on the ball. I don't particularly love it that way, but that is the way it has to be.

And that is the difference. That is Tommy Craig. No side he has been in has ever achieved anything. When you are watching a game it looks as if he is making a great contribution. But that is on the premise that what he is doing on the ball is what it is about at that level. And it is not. Maybe it should be. It would be nice if it were. But fashions and trends and styles are dictated by other necessities. The Second Division game is about graft, effort, hustling. Get the ball up in their box and challenge, challenge, challenge all over the field.

Now I don't agree with that. I think it is wrong. It is counter-productive, bad for the game. But the fact is that is the way it is. Until a manager comes along and gets a side to be successful playing the way Tommy Craig would like to play, and I would like to play, that is the way it is going to be. While you get Ron Saunders and people like that getting promotion, that is the way it is going to be. And Tommy Craig is going to be superfluous to that kind of football.

20 September

You can always judge how you stand with Benny by getting injured. He hates leaving out established players. Most times he'll play people even when they aren't fit. You get a pulled muscle, say, and you are a bit uneasy with it, and go at fifty-per-cent capacity. And Benny will nag you: 'Push it a bit harder', 'Have a real test', and get you up to 75–80-per-cent efficiency, then chuck you straight back in. Or he'll come into the treatment room when you've had a knock, glance at it and say 'Nothing wrong with that. It's all in the mind.'

On the other hand, if he's thinking of leaving you out, and glad of the opportunity, it's 'Now take your time. We don't want you rushing back, you might aggravate it. Give it a couple of weeks and make sure.' Although he's also crafty, and sometimes will say that, knowing that we will interpret it that way and so really rush back ourselves.

Recently, he hasn't been pushing Dennis to get fit. And he seems positively discouraging to Dougy Allder. When Dougy was injured at Fulham, Benny was really pushing. 'Nothing wrong with those ribs, son. You've got to be all right for next week.' But then he brought in Gordon Hill, and the crowd love the kid. So although Dougy is trying to get back, Benny is telling him to take it easy. He pulled him out of a practice game today, telling him he wasn't ready yet. 'You can't take any chances with cracked ribs.' Earlier he'd told Dougy they weren't cracked, just bruised.

And this is all crazy. Because Dougy is a really important member of the side.

21 September

We had a darts match last night. It's a rare get-together. Players don't get together much, and you don't have much time at the club to talk about football. But when you go out for an evening like that, conversation usually comes round to the game. And you talk about it at quite a deep level. As professionals you talk about it at a deeper level than you do with people outside the game. It isn't that people outside the game are necessarily less able to go along with the conversation, but it is more comfortable to talk with professionals because you can use your own verbal shorthand. You get to things quicker, and you understand one another.

I had a long conversation with Alf Wood. About discipline, and about the slackness at training. And Alf said 'The discipline is scandalous here. He should crack down, stop people taking liberties.'

I said 'Yeah, perhaps he should. But he gets it back in other ways. He lets people overstep the mark slightly; they get it back, though.'

With the type of people he has got at the club, if they take a liberty, they will know they have taken a liberty, and they will work that much harder in a crunch situation. I would say that Benny gets more effort over ninety minutes from us than any other club in the League.

And Alfie just said 'Rubbish. If you are going to run a club, you have got to have discipline. You cannot have people overweight . . .' Which is right.

Dennis is on the bench tomorrow. That's ridiculous. If he's fit, he should be in. I don't know what Benny is playing at. Dennis just shrugs. He doesn't seem very concerned. But he should be in the side.

22 September

Swindon 1   Millwall 3

Swindon are a bad side. A very bad side. They will be struggling at the bottom of the table before the season is over. A lot of young lads who cannot play, and a couple of older ones who don't want to play.

They went ahead after ten minutes. A poxy goal. A free kick, somebody nicked in, mis-hit it, and it was in the corner of the net. And then we started to play very very well for half an hour. We created about three or four scoring chances. We looked like we wanted to play. We looked the better side, the more skilful side. Just before half-time Clarky hit the post. Then we got a free kick, and Gordon put it straight in the back of the net. Great goal. Just the right time to score, and now we *know* we are a better side than them.

We went in at half-time. Everyone was pleased. Benny had not got much to say. We thought 'We can win this, no problem.'

We went out for the second half and scored straight away. Then we got a third goal within five minutes. Another great goal from Gordon, a great shot. He has not been playing well, so it was good to see him doing that.

Then we fell to bits. We stopped playing. They really came back at us, but they were so pathetic they could not even take advantage of us when we were playing so badly. We got very complacent. The last twenty-five minutes of the game we were rubbish. It could have been 6–1 really, but we did not finish them off.

Not only that, but we did not even do a good job of containing them. Kingy's troubles again came to the fore. He has not been doing his stuff in training. He is worried about this, worried about that, worried about getting away. A lot of problems for him. The system is against him. He is a talented lad, and he should be playing in the First Division, but he is not. So he is trying to fight the system, and in fighting it he is screwing himself up.

He dropped a few crosses in the second half, but anyway we got away with it.

After the game I was sick. I walked in the dressing-room utterly disgusted. Disgusted with the way we played, the lack of professionalism, the lack of honesty, the lack of respect for the game.

But of course Benny was delighted. Everyone was beaming, smiling. And I muttered. A few mutters. I muttered at Benny, I muttered at some of the lads 'Rubbish. We'll get slaughtered if we play like this again.'

Nobody took much notice. Everybody was saying 'They are not a bad side. We won. Two points, that is all that matters.'

But it is not all that matters. There is more to it than that.

25 September

A really unusual five-a-side this morning. Five-a-sides are great. It's really a good relaxation after the hard work, but useful too. They seem to go in cycles. Sometimes they are serious; sometimes they are just fun. But always there are certain conventions. You always have a scapegoat. Normally it's in good fun, with sarcastic remarks like 'Oh, you're playing a blinder.' Often the scapegoat is selected before the game starts; long before it can be seen that anyone is having a bad time. Sometimes it can be bad. When the stars have one of their 'serious stuff' moods, they'll often pick on an apprentice and make his life a misery from the moment he makes a mistake. Which is bad. It can ruin a kid, because they can be really cruel.

There are some people who always mess around – me, Gordon Bolland,

Brownie. Alan gets really mad sometimes, because he is one of the people who always tries 100 per cent. So does Brian Clark. He's a really good pro. Been around all these years, been to a lot of clubs, and still full of enthusiasm. Loves the game, loves training, loves five-a-sides. He gives everything at all times.

Which made this morning very unusual. He had a nightmare. Couldn't do a thing right. I started giving him the normal treatment. 'Why don't you get in the bath?', 'Clark, you berk' – that sort of thing. At one stage he couldn't take any more, and came after me: 'I'm going to kill you, you little sod.' Which is really out of character. I couldn't understand it. Normally you just give chat back. Stevie Brown is a favourite scapegoat. And he'll give it all back with interest. 'Bottler' he calls me. 'Bottler,' he yells at me. 'Never made a tackle in your life. Bottle it.' But here was Brian taking it to heart.

I apologized to him later. He said he was sorry too, and said he was upset because his father was ill. You wonder how often players or crowds ever think about those sort of worries when they get on to someone having a bad time. 'Rubbish' is easy to shout, but most people don't think that players have ordinary lives with ordinary fears and worries. We're expected, and expect one another to some extent, to be automatons.

Five-a-sides apart, we still aren't training properly. It's difficult to pin down what's wrong, but there's just a lack of concentration, a lackadaisical atmosphere. But with three wins on the trot, everyone is sure it's OK, we are on our way and don't need to work.

I spent a lot of the weekend thinking about what Alfie said last week. After our performance at Swindon, I'm sure he is right. I was arguing emotionally, because I believe in Benny. I like him and trust him. But Alfie was being rational. We do need discipline. People are getting away with murder. And it showed in that terrible second-half performance at Swindon.

Having had three results on the trot, we are really in a good position to work positively on our weaker aspects. Again, it is the coaching and organization which is at fault. We do these functions, but they are not realistic. We are vulnerable to teams throwing their full backs in at us, and we are bad at closing teams up. When Dennis and Dougy were together with me and Gordon Bolland in midfield we worked out for ourselves how to do it. But at the moment we are all going our separate ways. We aren't good as a unit at putting pressure on the other team. We all want to get the ball back, when they have got it, but we are all going our separate ways. Whereas if you attack the ball as a group you have a hell of a chance of getting it back. If someone goes in as an individual, he will sell himself and get beaten. But if you've got the team doing it, everyone getting behind the ball, and someone supporting him when he goes in, that is how you get the ball back.

But we don't practise that in training. Lawrie talks a lot, instead of setting up situations. And for young lads like Gordon Hill or Stevie Brown, who are inexperienced and not thinkers about the game anyway, that is hopeless. It just goes in one ear and out the other. If you took them out on to the pitch, within two minutes you could show them what you want. That is what coaching is. It is the difference between working on the game and talking about the game.

It is the same with full backs coming in at us. If the opposition keeper has the ball and can throw it to his full backs, they bring it, or knock it along the line and we are fighting for the ball in our half. So you want to stop that. So all you have to do, and this is a simple coaching point, is to throw your wingers on to their full backs. So the keeper gets the ball, looks up, and everybody is picked up. So all he can do is bash it down field. Where Alan or Kitch wins it and knocks it back. Then we are fighting for the ball in their half, as opposed to ours. A simple matter of organization. But it is the difference between winning a game and losing a game. And that is the sort of thing we ought to be working on. Because we might get away with it against Wednesday and Swindon or Hull, but against the good sides it is that sort of thing which is vital.

27 September

We went to Deptford Park again this morning. Really it is an ideal place. There is an all-weather surface most managers would give their right arm for. We go there the whole time, though, and tend to get a bit fed up with it. Particularly those of us, like Dennis, who feel we should be doing different sorts of training, rather than just running and five-a-sides. He is always complaining that we do too much running and not enough ballwork; and that we don't get on grass enough with our boots on. I agree with him about not doing enough ballwork. But the Redgra versus grass issue always seems to me to be overstated by Dennis. Certainly using Redgra exclusively is bad. Both because variety is essential in training; and because although we can have a reasonable seven- or eight-a-side game on the Redgra pitch, there are some things you need the real situation for. And Redgra does demand different skills to an extent. Even having studs on rather than slippers makes a difference. But I don't think that is the real issue. It's more the kind of functions we do and the kind we should do; and the running versus working with the ball issues. They are the important ones.

If Dennis and Benny had a normal manager–captain relationship things would be easier. Dennis could go and tell him we were worried about the kind of training we do, and something would be done about it. A manager should respond. But Benny, who is always thinking Dennis is a threat to him and never wanting to be seen to bow down to him, won't have it. And Dennis always brings it up in the dressing-room in front of the lads, rather than going up to see Benny quietly. He did again this morning. 'We going to Deptford today for a change?' he asked as soon as Benny came in.

So we went over there. And Dennis won't train. We did these six long 'doggies'. Which means you run for about a minute flat out; rest for thirty seconds; then go again. Four of you go at once. It's virtually a race between the four of you, although not a race as such. The real opponent is the clock. But Dennis just strolls it, while everyone else is bursting their lungs. Benny stood there watching, grim-faced. But he said nothing to Dennis. Lawrie yelled 'Come on, Dennis. Come on, Dennis!' But Dennis ignores him completely. Insolence really. It happens all the time. We're almost immune to it now. If Dennis doesn't agree with something, he doesn't do it. Which is wrong. Gordon, Harry and I don't agree with a lot of the training either. But if Benny says go to the Redgra at Deptford, you have to go. You've got to train. And you have to do the hard work, the running against the clock.

There are some things you can dodge, like exercises. If you are doing stomach exercises, or stretches, you can duck if you want. Instead of keeping your knees straight, you can bend them. No one will see you. But if you duck in the hard work, you stick out like a sore thumb. It's blatant.

Sometimes we do overtaking laps. You run round the park, and while the rest of the group is jogging, three or four of you go off ahead, and race round the park to catch the others up again. But Dennis trots at his own pace. If he goes first with three others, they will pass him in the first twenty-five yards. And we all have to wait for him to get round at his own pace.

No other player could get away with it. The lads all wait for Benny to hammer him. And Benny won't do anything about it. It is one of the quirks of the club. It is one of those things that nags at you. Nags and nags and nags.

It doesn't affect us in a real sense. It isn't even the fact that Dennis might let you down because he is not fit. It's just that it shatters the unity of the place. Because the one thing you need for unity is the feeling that everyone is setting out on the same level. The same restraints, and the same degree of permissiveness about the taking of liberties. And once you start showing favouritism one way or another it begins to wreck things. Because it gives everyone else an excuse. Even the bad people who don't train are given an excuse by the laxity allowed Dennis.

And it affects anyone who is wavering. Training is not really a matter of whether you are a good guy or a bad guy so much as whether you can motivate yourself on a cold Thursday morning or not. With some lads it is a borderline decision. They may not be great ones for punishing themselves, but if they see everyone else punishing themselves, if they are in a work atmosphere, they will do it. But if the captain of the club messes about, they will take it a little bit easier. They won't be as outrageous as him. But when it gets to the point where they have to push themselves, they will think 'Oh, what the hell . . .' and take it a bit easy. And that is the real harm it is doing. It bothers all the lads.

But at the same time you laugh about it. You laugh at Benny for allowing it, because he lets himself down so badly. There can't be more than half a dozen clubs in the country where a player could do it and still be club captain. He is a strange man, Benny. A very complex character. We don't understand how he can allow it, because it is his job which is at stake ultimately.

28 September

We have Carlisle at the Den tomorrow. Another home win, and we will be really up there in the top five. And the best part of the season for us is yet to come. But there is a bad atmosphere, a lazy atmosphere, a kind of brooding greyness hanging over the place.

What we are doing is going to Crystal Palace on Mondays. We get changed, and finally start around 10.45. We have ten minutes running around doing exercises. Then we have twelve-a-side because the apprentices are there too. Two-touch football on a very narrow pitch. So everyone kicks the ball into each other's balls, and it is over the roof and all over the shop. I'm in goal one end, Gordon Bolland is in goal the other. So one whole morning – nothing. On Tuesday we go out and run our cobs off for half an hour, then we get the ball and play five-a-side. So again, nothing. Wednesday we have off. So there seems to be nobody really interested in correcting our basic faults, in working at the game.

The balance of the side is not right yet either. We have got a kid playing outside left who is not ready yet. Dennis is sitting on the bench tomorrow, which is ridiculous. He is one of our more positive players. It is obvious that without him we are not such a good side as we are with him. It is only a matter of time, until we lose a game, and then Benny will put him in. Then Benny will say 'Now we are back to our best. This is us.'

But I cannot understand why he does not do it now. Why do we have to lose before we pull ourselves together? Why not work and organize ourselves now?

29 September

Millwall 1   Carlisle United 2

'No way can we lose this game. Carlisle never beat us at home. Not many sides do, but certainly not the Carlisles of this world.' That was what we went out thinking. It was just a matter of waiting for the goal to come. We will get the first goal, and then start playing a bit, and the other one or two will come. We've done it a hundred times, we've done it two hundred times. Same old thing; dead easy.

They were desperate. They had lost at home, they had lost everywhere. They lost one game 6–0. So we started off. The pitch was bumpy, and it was very windy. In the first quarter of an hour we had one, maybe two, chances. Just little flurries, but nothing occurred. We were all kind of suspended in mid-air. No one was doing anything. But we were not worried. 'We will get a chance, and it will be in the back of the net.'

We did not respect them. A lot of them were just waiting for us to score. But there was one little guy in midfield who was working his heart out. Positive, making runs, tackling, jumping, getting involved. He seemed to be one of the few players on their side who wanted to play. I just looked at him and thought 'Ten out of ten for effort, but you are wasting your time.'

So half-time came and it was 0–0. We were kicking into our favourite end in the second half. We had got the wind as well. Everything was right. A couple more near misses. Alfie missed an absolute sitter. That should have been the first goal.

Sides do not lose at the Den; they commit suicide. They wait for you to score. They offer you the game on a plate. Carlisle had offered us the game on a plate, but we had not taken it.

Now there was uneasiness, the first hint of doubt; a bit of desperation crept in. Alfie's miss was crucial. You think 'That's ominous. We won't get an easier chance than that. This is not going to be the day.'

They began to see that there was nothing to be afraid of. They were beginning to play a little bit more. They were beginning to think they could win. And we were beginning to realize we could fail to win. And then we thought 'We will switch it on.' But we could not. It just got worse and worse. In the middle of the second half it just got unbelievable. Nobody could pass the ball, nobody could find it, nobody wanted the ball, nobody wanted to do anything at all positive. People were putting their heads on their chest, and looking around, blaming other people. And everybody was getting edgy.

Then, ten minutes from the end, Brownie – he is overweight and having a nightmare – *blasts* a ball back to Kingy. Kingy had no chance. It flew past him, hit the post, and came back into his arms. He turned round and lashed it upfield. One of their defenders headed it out, Gordon hit it first time, and it was in the back of the net.

I could not even raise my arms. I was embarrassed. We did not deserve it. I did not do a war dance. I just stood there and said 'Well, thank Christ for that! We have got away with it again.' Everyone was pleased now, it was a matter of holding out for eight or nine minutes. Well, we did not even think in terms of holding out. We thought 'That's it, it is over.' We knocked it about for five minutes. They had jacked it in, except for that last desperate spurt every away team makes.

Some guy hit an aimless ball into the box. Kitch – there was not an opponent near him – headed it back to Kingy. But Kingy had come out instead of staying on his line, hadn't given Kitch a call, and it was in the back of the net. It bounced twice, and we thought Kingy had it. Always gets those balls, he is good at it. But not this time. It was Kingy's fault basically. Because he did not shout. Again it is all part of this thing he has been going through. It's predictable. You knew it had to happen some time. But you never thought . . . And now it is 1–1. Christ! I held my head in my hands and thought 'This is unbelievable!'

And this paralysing feeling came over me. There was no answer to it. So anyway, we had dropped a point. We got a little desperate, but I knew we would not get it now. There was no real desire to win.

Now they were steaming, Carlisle. They could not believe it. Energy! Positive runs! They were calling for the ball; they were knocking it around; they were ten feet tall. Transformation. To come to Millwall and get a point!

So they boot a ball upfield, a fellow gets it, Kingy comes tearing out of his box, scythes the winger down. For no apparent reason. Free kick. Fellow takes it. The centre half has come up, heads it, it hits Kitch and then the back of the net. In the net!

I looked around again. I could not believe it. It really was like a bad dream. It is impossible to lose at home to Carlisle any time, but having been 1–0 up with ten minutes to go, it was unbelievable.

We went off and got in the bath. We had been diabolical. We had produced the kind of football that our training had threatened all season. Inept, grey, sterile, nothing football. No energy, nothing.

Nobody said anything. We just sat there, disbelief on everybody's face. Muttering about Kingy, muttering about this, muttering about that. And I was angry. I had not played well. I was annoyed at that. But I was not so much annoyed because we had not played well, but because the signs had been there for a good two weeks.

I don't like getting drunk, but tonight I feel 'I'm going to get drunk.' There is nothing else for it.

I have never felt ashamed about Millwall until today. I have felt proud about them always. The character, the skill, the results we have got away from home . . . you are proud to play for Millwall. You think 'What a good set of lads. What a good club to play for.' But this . . . it was such a waste. To get beaten like that!

30 September

So I came home last night and had a few drinks. But it doesn't help. When you wake up in the morning, you think 'It didn't happen' or you try to block it out. But it happened. And when you read the Sunday papers you soon learn that it did.

Sunday is very much a down day anyway. You build up all week emotionally and physically to Saturday. You get really wound up, then bang! Saturday afternoon it all comes out. Even the games that look diabolical to people watching, games where nothing has been achieved, nothing creative anyway, you come off the park thinking 'Gotta get in that bath. Jesus!' You have put everything into it physically and emotionally, oblivious of the fact that it is drivel. And by Sunday you are no good for anything.

When you've won, it isn't so bad. Alan and I both have this routine of getting the Sunday papers, looking at the League table, working out who is playing who next week, where it will leave us – 'five points behind, but if they lose it'll only be three', all that sort of thing. But when you've lost like we did yesterday, when even you are conscious you've been in a load of rubbish, the Sunday papers you do not need.

1 October

This morning everyone seemed to have forgotten last Saturday. We are at Sheffield on Wednesday, Forest on Saturday, and the feeling is 'Well, we'll try and nick something there.'

The lads are sick, I suppose, in their own way. But footballers are resilient. They bounce back quickly as a group. Jokes, birds, you talk about anything. Even football. Some of the lads do anyway. When you get older you start talking about the game a bit, seeing things you never saw before, feeling responsible for things you never felt responsible for before. It becomes more difficult to shrug things off.

So we started training. A bit of running to get warmed up, then we were going to have this practice match. Lawrie was handing the bibs out. And he walked past me. 'That is very odd of him.' I thought nothing of it; just a little bit perturbed. I looked after him, and he was giving out first-team shirts. And he was giving one to Robin Wainwright . . . and he gave one to Dennis . . . and I looked around . . . 'I'm dropped! No! But I am!'

I could not believe it. I could not think for a minute. And Benny was standing there as if nothing had happened. No one said anything to me.

He had given me a reserve shirt. 'Play in midfield,' he said. How do you react? It was like somebody had plunged a dagger in my back. I was so hurt. Not so much because I was dropped, but because they had done it like that.

And they could not do it to me! I was choked. I had been playing reasonably well; certainly better than a lot of other people. And I cared! I was part of it. This was me, this was the lads. And then BANG! I'm out of it.

So he said 'Let's have the first-team lads over here. You lot go and have a kick about at the far end.' So they had all gone away, the lads, for a team talk. And I went up the other end with the youngsters. I could not believe it.

I could feel tears welling up in my eyes, but I thought 'Nah, that's no good.' So I just stood there for about five or ten minutes. I don't know how long it was. I can't remember how long the talk went on. The young lads were knocking it about, and I looked round, and there was this little group, and Benny was talking to them. And you feel so left out.

And there's the hurt. It just happens. A snap of the fingers, and you are gone. Out. All the commitment, all the emotion, all the hard work, all the belief. Everything gone. Because some idiot fooled around at the back in the last eight minutes on Saturday.

And my first reaction then was to walk out. There and then. But I thought 'No, anybody can be dropped. Now you have got to show you are a man. Now you have got to show you are big.'

So I made a few jokes with the young lads, picked my chin up, and started playing this practice game. I did my best, I worked hard, and funnily enough I started playing really well. Because again there was this strange feeling of relief. 'Sod it. I'm out of it.' So I just enjoyed myself for half an hour. And all the time, at the back of my mind, I was wondering 'What am I going to do? How am I going to react? What do I do now?'

Seven games of the season had gone. And after all the struggle, all the worry, all the dreams, you are on the scrapheap. That is what the reserves is, when you are twenty-eight. No one had said a word to me. It was the same as if I had never given a damn. They had treated me as if I had never tried.

And I *had* tried. In the games where Dennis had been out, and there was no one there to take responsibility, I had taken it. I had covered for people, I had worked, I had shouted, I had bawled, I had grafted, I had tackled – which I cannot do very well – I had done all of that. And I was missing Dennis being alongside me doing things, because he takes a lot of that responsibility. I took all that on my own shoulders, tried to do the right thing, tried to do more than my whack, to make up for the fact that he was not there. All the time waiting for him to get back into the side so we could get it organized again. Like we had done in the latter part of last season. It never entered my mind that I might be dropped.

It had, funnily enough, when Franky had been playing so well. I thought 'Well, Dennis is going to come back in, and he just might drop me.' But then I had played well in a couple of games, I had made the goal against Wednesday, and I had played well in the first half at Swindon when things were rocky. I had pulled the side together, and I thought I had done very well. So I said to myself 'Now it's OK. You won't be dropped.' I thought he would drop Gordon Hill. I wanted Dennis back in the side.

But he had dropped Gordon Hill and me. And he brought this lad Robin Wainwright in. He has done well in the reserves, and should be given a chance. But he is not a midfield player, he is a winger or a striker.

So I reacted by playing as best I could for the reserves in that practice match. Trying to be manly, trying not to be small-minded. And when we finished I went to see Benny. When I walked through the door he said 'What do you want?'

'You know what I want,' I said. 'I want to leave this place. I want to leave within a week. I'm finished here.'

'Out of the question,' he said. 'You're too good a player.'

So I said 'I don't care why you have dropped me, I don't want to discuss it. Team selection is your business. But I'm finished with it. I have put too much work in, too much commitment, too much caring to be messed around like that. You did not even tell me before that I was dropped. I find out when a guy walks past me with a shirt. That's you, that is this club. No more for me. I'm finished. I want to leave. And if you do not let me leave, I'll leave anyway.'

'Out of the question. Calm yourself down.'

I did not talk about why he had dropped me. I do not believe in discussing team selection with managers. They have got a reason, and whatever the reason is, it is good enough. It is their job. You don't have to take it, if you don't believe it is right.

I was in a terrible temper. My hand was shaking, I could not talk properly. I was hurt more than angry.

So I said 'I'll wait ten days. And if you don't let me go, I'll go anyway. Don't put me on the sheet, don't take me with you.'

'What about the money?'

'You can stuff the money,' I said. 'I don't care about that.'

So I went home. I phoned Sandra first, and told her what had happened. I walked in and just burst out crying. I sat here for quarter of an hour, and I just cried.

I had never cried before about football. Never ever. But this time I did. I don't know why. Maybe it was the hurt, the injustice of it. But that has happened before. Every year, the first sign of the team having problems and it is me he drops. He tells me that he thinks the world of me as a person, but when we lose games the first person he sorts out is me. I do think he likes me. I think the reason he does drop me every time is because of a weakness in him. He is the kind of person who would sooner hurt his friends than his enemies. But I did not think it would happen to me again.

The other lads were surprised. Alan said 'It's scandalous.'

I had not looked for sympathy. When you get dropped, players come up to you and say 'Diabolical.' They always say it whether they mean it or not. But when it happens to me, I try and avoid them. I don't want them to say it, because it does not mean anything. It is not real. What is real is what goes on the teamsheet. The rest is rubbish.

2 October

Being dropped is something everyone in the game has to face. Manchester United dropped Bobby Charlton once. How do you face it? Yesterday I came home and I just cried! We went into Bromley in the afternoon shopping. But it's eating into you the whole time. You can't think about anything else for one minute. You go home and you are restless, edgy.

The whole time you are thinking 'What am I going to do?' I was in great doubt whether I should go to the ground today, or stay away. I didn't know what to do. Whether to jack it all in again, or go. Maybe go in for the money, sit on the bench as twelfth man, which means a lot extra on your wages. Or say 'Stuff the money' and keep out of it altogether.

But I went in this morning, and had a long chat with Benny. He called me into his office. He was hovering around me all morning, which is what he does when he knows you have got the needle with him. He called me into his room and said 'Have you changed your mind about going on the teamsheet? Do you still not want to be in it?'

So I said 'Leave me out. See how you do.' I said I wanted no part of it. I'm not going to sit on the bench or in the stand, tearing my guts out every week, wanting them to win in one sense, but basically wanting them to lose, because I cannot get back into the side until they lose. But he said 'Come as thirteenth man; and get your money. Don't be a fool to yourself.' So in the end I agreed.

4 October

Sheffield Wednesday 3   Millwall 2

So we went up to Sheffield. I wasn't on the bench, I went as thirteenth man. You go into the dressing-room before the game, and you smile and say 'All the best, lads.' What does that mean? If they do well you stay out. And when they get beaten, as we did last night, what do you do? You act. Because you can't come in with a big smile all over your face saying 'Great. Now you've been beaten I can get back in.' Everybody else is sick. But you aren't. You are pleased. So you come in and make faces; pretend that you are sick like the rest of them. But everyone knows that you are acting.

I sat in the stand with John Sissons, who is injured. I was sitting among some Millwall supporters too. They were all saying 'Cor, you not in, Eamon? What a liberty! He should have dropped someone else.' You can't say anything. And they say the same to everyone when they are dropped. Some of them mean it, some don't.

The game was a shambles. Terrible. First half was diabolical. Kingy kept like a clown, gave away two goals. And he was being watched by Manchester City. Their scout left before the end. But while they are out there what am I doing? I'm sitting in the stand, wanting them to lose, but unable to show it. Because there are people around, I've got to pretend to want them to win. I can't jump up in the air when Sheffield score. Which I want to do. And when Millwall score I'm sick, but I have to jump up in the air. And there is this terrible conflict the whole time. And it is the same for everybody who is dropped.

You are always pleased when they have been beaten, because it means you are a candidate again. You are sick for the lads, of course, but your predominant emotion is delight.

I went into the dressing-room afterwards. People were throwing their boots off disconsolately, swearing a lot. I looked at Dennis. He shrugged his shoulders. He wasn't surprised. He looked as if he was past caring. Another confirmation for him of what he thinks about Millwall. I couldn't look at Alan. He is my closest friend, but I couldn't go to him. Because I was still isolated. I had not been part of the defeat. You aren't just isolated from the good things when you're out of the side, but from the bad things too. The lads who played and Benny are sharing the gloom, just as it would be their joy to share if they had done well. So I kept quiet. I sat down and read the programme for the fiftieth time, and tried to grab half a cup of tea. There was me, Benny and Jack while the lads were having their baths. Benny was walking around shaking his head. There was nothing he wanted to say to me; and nothing I wanted to say to him. He went to the mirror to comb his hair, as he always does before having to go and face the directors' room.

Now that's another tough situation. It's always tough for a manager to face that when his team has lost. It is not so much facing your own directors. That comes later. It is the guests and the opposition directors and other managers saying 'Unlucky' and not meaning it.

For the reserve, after about half an hour, when you've helped Jack Blackman get all the gear together, it isn't so bad. By then the lads have forgotten the game and you are all one again. Particularly for an away game like Sheffield, where you are staying overnight. You go off and have a few beers together. And you can feel part of it.

But Benny put a curfew on. So we didn't go out, just had a drink in the hotel lounge. There was a pretty bad atmosphere really.

What does a manager do? Benny could say 'Go on, have a few beers and please yourself.' But it is difficult.

If I was a manager, I would tend to think there was no use in punishing people if they have done their best. And at Millwall they invariably have done their best. Let them go out and have a few beers, win or lose. But it is early season. We have a game on Saturday, so we have got to keep ourselves reasonably fit. The danger is that the lads could go out and drink a lot, pull a few birds and it ends as a four-in-the-morning job. And then you travel back the next day, so there is only Friday to recover.

But I think that players feel much more responsible nowadays than they did. There are far fewer cheats around. Certainly not at Millwall, which is one of the greatest things about the place. Over the years I've played there, one of the greatest joys has been that they have had no bad people. The one or two that came Benny got out quickly. We've always had good lads.

I've seen a few bad ones elsewhere. Going away with the Irish team there have been lads over the years who don't care whether they win or lose. They are looking for something else out of it: the 'big time'.

There is an element of that left in the game, but it is going very quickly. One thing I've always hated is the image of the hard-drinking, hard-living professional sportsman who goes out and stomps all over the world. That was part of the game when I first came into it in Manchester. I remember going out with a couple of the other players one Friday night to the dogs, then on to a nightclub. We were playing the next day, and I was really worried, guilty. And they said 'Nothing to worry about. This is what it is all about.' And to a large extent at that time it was. Particularly in Manchester, there were a lot of playboys around and a lot of places to go. But there is not a lot of that left in football now.

And that has been one of the joys at Millwall. Players are honest. And Benny is normally good. He lets the players go out more often than not. And I think that is right. If a player goes out on a Wednesday night and even if he gets drunk out of his mind, if he is a good pro he will know what he has done. He will make up for it on the Saturday. He will give you that much more because he had that licence on Wednesday.

Last season we played Everton in the Cup. We went to Torquay for four days beforehand. It is a fantastic place down there for nightlife. It was in January. London was terrible. But down there it was really nice. A warm atmosphere and a carefree air about the place. It was quiet, because it was out of season, but there was still a fairly hectic social life.

The first couple of days we were down there we went out. Benny was really good and took the leash off. We found a club and had a few drinks. We did not really look after ourselves for those four days. We took liberties. On the Thursday we went back to London to go up to Everton.

I think Benny knew we had stayed up late and drunk more than we should have done. And I think he had done it to relax us. We went out and played like fury. We fought and we battled. It was a hell of a game, and we got a hell of a result.

So we asked if we could go to Torquay before the next round. Benny said yes, so before we played Wolves we went down there again and had a ball. We played really well again at Wolves, even though we lost.

These were isolated instances of us taking liberties. You could not do it every week and get away with it. But if you have got good lads it proves you can let them off the leash, and they will still produce the goods. Especially if you pick the right time.

5 October

Lawrie did it again with his damn bibs this morning. We were having a five-a-side. On Friday mornings the first team normally play the reserves in little five-a-sides. And Lawrie gave me a first-team jersey, and gave Robin Wainwright a reserve-team jersey. Of course I thought I was back in the side and Robin thought he was dropped. So Robin naturally was really angry, and he couldn't get it together, and it destroyed him. I was angry too, because I did not want to come back like that. I knew it wasn't fair that he should be dropped after one game in which he had not done badly. And I knew that the lads would not think it fair either. It was really eating me. I played for half an hour, stumbling all over the place, confused, wondering what was going on. And Robin is confused too. I can see his face and the lad is so choked. He has had one game after being at the club for ten months. And then they drop him like this.

I looked at him at the end of practice as if to say 'Sorry, son, I think it is a liberty, but what can you do?'

So we went back to the ground, and Benny put up the teamsheet. And I wasn't playing. Robin was still in. So I made a beeline for Lawrie and said 'What the hell were you playing at with those bibs? You give me a first-team jersey, and Robin a reserve one?'

'Oh,' said Lawrie, 'that was just coincidence. I gave the vest to you because you were standing nearest to me.'

Just a simple little thing, but that really hurt. It shows how you can be treated in this game. In the course of a morning you are in and out of the side with a snap of the fingers. Because you are told nothing, you have to watch for signs all the time. And then someone's incredible unthinking action destroys a morning for you.

6 October

Nottingham Forest 3   Millwall 0

Now we are in the depths. Today Franky Saul got sent off. Stupidity. He deserved to be sent off. They are a pretty moderate side, who we play again on Wednesday in the League Cup. And we will beat them. We have got the needle with them, because they were 1–0 up when Franky was sent off and not playing well. But when they got us down to ten men in the second half, they started taking the mickey, and buzzing around, and doing all sorts of things. Dennis said to one of them on the way off 'You had better save some of that energy for Wednesday night.' Because they are going to need it. That is the incentive we need to knock them out of the League Cup. We will be steaming from the start.

Franky felt diabolical afterwards. From the stand I thought it was quite right that he was sent off. He had had a go, stuck the nut on a fellow, for which he was booked. Then he went in very late a few minutes afterwards. There was nothing else the referee could have done. But he was raging.

You have to sympathize, because the implications of being sent off are so bad. You lose a lot of money, missing three games, and you could lose your place in the side as a result. I think Franky thought that if he was going to be sent off anyway, he wished he had done the fellow properly. There's nothing worse than being sent off when you haven't really done any damage. You feel you might as well have done some.

The lads felt we had done all right until Franky was sent off. That was the turning point. So everyone was fairly angry. I've never seen a case where players say it was right someone was sent off. It's very hard to see your own fellows in a bad light. Unless someone has thrown a killer punch and caught the other guy on the point of the chin, you never feel it is right.

It is a horrible thing, the long walk. You go in alone, and the old boy (every club has this old boy) comes in and unlocks the dressing-room door for you, and sympathizes. Franky came and sat on the bench afterwards. He was fuming all the game.

Alfie and Dennis in particular were furious. It was another confirmation for them of the troubles we have been having with referees. The lads felt he shouldn't have been sent off. I thought he should. But I was sitting in the stand. A non-combatant, a rational critic. That is the thing about being thirteenth man. You are watching the game through reasonable eyes. And that has got nothing to do with football or any other sport.

So the lads have the needle with Forest. The general feeling was disgust at them. Because until we went one down, they had not looked anything. They had looked a load of bottlers really. Dennis was very angry. He said 'We'll stuff them on Wednesday night.'

But then, where do we go from here? By beating them we will be reacting to something that happened today. It won't be something we have created ourselves.

Before the season started I said this was going to be a cataclysmic year for Millwall. Either way. And it is, I think, beginning to happen now. We have got guys in the side overweight. You have got the keeper who is in a terrible situation because of his contract. And it looks to me as if he has blown his chance now. Manchester City have watched him twice – today and last Wednesday – and both times they have walked out before the end. A £100,000 buy, and he is making mistakes. Elementary mistakes. It is not the lad's fault. He is in a diabolical situation. He is trapped. People react stupidly, they make mistakes, they get desperate. I have tried to tell him ... but he can't help it. He talks to journalists, he makes these ridiculous statements to the papers.

You could say he is childish, but he is desperate. He feels his whole life's ambition – to play in the First Division – within his grasp. And there is nothing he can do to realize it. He has worked hard for it for four years. Brave, skilful, competent at his job, great at his job, and it has not happened. He must look at our side, and see this shambles we have been for the last month – the last three games anyway; it seems like a month – and despair. It has only been a week. We had won our previous three games; it seems like a month since then.

Alf walked in after the match today, and said 'I wish I would break my leg!' He is sick, sick about the club, sick about the way he sees it run. Because he thinks about it a little bit. So am I sick.

That is what hurts more than anything. A good club, a good side, we should walk away with this League. With Dougy in the side . . . a great little player, Dougy, always done well for us, always does a good job. And he dropped him. Bang! Out! Now Dougy has broken his ribs in the reserves. He dropped Dougy and played this kid. Then Dennis got injured, and he left him out for three weeks.

He has destroyed it; destroyed the delicate balance. We went through nine months of last season as one of the most successful sides in the Division; seven or eight months, anyway, from October onwards. And he has taken all that for granted and destroyed that delicate thing. He thinks that you can muck around with the mechanism of a team, and still come up with the same answers. And you cannot. It is delicate. Take one or two players out of a side, move one or two players around, and you have ruined the whole thing.

Everybody was moody on the coach coming home tonight. The directors were moody, Benny was moody. There were bad vibes all round.

Basically you are all in it for the glory. And glory is not something you share. It is your glory. You only achieve it together. But you don't share it. Everyone sets out to achieve it, and the team is your means to that end. The togetherness is your means to achieve it, but once you achieve it, it's yours. Relationships in a football team are tenuous. They are not true friendships – very rarely, anyway. It's more a shared experience, on a not very deep basis. Of course most friendships are based on common ground, shared experiences. But in football these days, shared experience means shared money.

When the bad times come, it is every man for himself. Unless there is very good leadership. If not the relationships begin to crack up. Because sport is basically a lonely thing for every individual in it, even in team sports. Teams are basically individuals. A group of individuals.

You talk about team spirit and being together. But you always find in practice, when the bad times come, the cracks come, it's every man for himself. Because there is glory and money and your career at stake. And that entails backbiting, snidiness, scapegoating and a whole host of other things.

7 October

Watching two games from the stand has been really instructive. Seeing the Second Division as it really is. It is a much less complex thing than one thinks when one is playing. You go out to play Forest, who really are terrible. But before you go out, and when you are out there, you're thinking in terms of this tremendous task. 'Christ, we've got to beat these.'

Sitting in the stand, out of it all, cool and objective, you see the game in a different light. You realize just how many balls go astray. You see so many players trying to do really difficult things. The full back will have the ball. He's got a simple ball on, and a very difficult ball on. Now here is a player in the Second Division. A good player with a fair amount of ability, but no genius. Winfield of Forest, for example. A good player, but not a great player. He can strike the ball well. If he has got someone thirty yards away who is free, he will hit him nine times out of ten. Most professionals can. But put him in a situation where there is a little bit of pressure, and he is not content with that.

There were twenty-two players out there on Wednesday. Four or five were doing the simple things. The rest of them – the ball was flying all over the place. You would get a lad in space. He would get the ball played to his feet forwards. And he would try to turn unbelievably quickly and knock a ball under pressure. Pressure that he only imagined. There was no one near him. He was so used to thinking like that, instead of controlling it, looking up and playing a simple ball. He was doing things in his head at ninety miles an hour. The worst thing that has happened to my game in the last two years is that I've lost my composure. What I was good at was putting my foot on the ball, and knocking it around. Doing the simple things well, and slowing it down.

Part of the problem is getting older. You get to know the game better, and you get to feel more responsible for things. You start to feel you can influence things. That's great. But it is also dangerous. You start trying to do things that are not within your scope. And you start feeling responsible for things that aren't your responsibility.

This happens partly because lads know, especially in the lower divisions, that the one thing that keeps them in the game is their application. Their dedication. The intensity with which they approach the game. Which leads them to this feeling that they have got to go out and punish themselves for ninety minutes. This is crucial to players, particularly in the lower divisions. It is one of the most important things in the game at the moment – the idea that you somehow have to suffer.

That is what really distinguishes English football – the amount of people willing to do that. And that is what also destroys English football. On the continent, or in the First Division, you get fellows who feel they don't have to do that in the same way. They will do it on the ball. They will take responsibility and play. It takes as much courage to play, to get on the ball and be composed.

All of those lads out here yesterday were honest. That was the one distinguishing feature. Of twenty-two on the field, sixteen or eighteen, the great majority, were totally honest. Within a certain definition of honesty, which is: 'Run your cobs off, whack everything you see, and then chase it.'

Carlisle in many ways are the best side I've seen. In many respects they were crap. But they had two things going for them: simplicity and honesty. They were never going to give in.

They weren't technically a good side. They had a few players who could play. But there must be sixteen or eighteen sides in the Second Division with more. Balderstone is a tremendous, gifted player, and they played off him. They are one of the better footballing sides in the simple things. They did try to play.

And Les O'Neill is unbelievable. He is useless if you use any of the textbook criteria. All he has got is a heart as big as the Den. A real human dynamo, as they say in Fleet Street. He kept them going. They were dead and he would not stop. He was kicking and fighting and chasing.

Well, he can play a little bit. But it's his tremendous character that distinguishes him. Living proof of the triumph of the spirit. There are definitely fifty better midfield players in the Second Division. But I will bet none of them have a good game against him. Because he sickens you. At the end of the game you feel 'Well, thank God he is off my back at last!' You were sick of him. He never left you alone.

He never gave it away when he had it. And he never left you alone when you got it. He was up your backside the whole time. Not dirty, but biting, fighting, niggling, chasing. If he couldn't get up and head it, he would get up and put off the fellow who was going to head it. And as soon as he got it he gave it to the nearest man. Simple. He never gave it back to you. He was like Nobby Stiles when he was playing well. A pain in the ass. And that is the greatest thing in the lower divisions.

Or in any division. Leeds, for example. What a terrible team to play against. A pain. You try and take a throw-in. They have got everybody picked up, a man in front of the winger, and a man on you. You can't even take a throw-in. It demoralizes you. After half an hour you think 'Oh hell, we can't even take a throw-in and get the ball.' It is terrible, especially for skilful midfield players. There you are, a skilful player, and you can't get the ball. So you start trying that bit more desperately. Then you get this throw-in. And you still have no chance. There used to be no question. It was at your feet and away you went. Not now. Not against good sides. They have got everyone picked up. Everyone. That is what the coaches are telling everyone to do.

Now that is very unimportant in one sense. But in another sense it is crucial. Because you are taking your throw-in. A throw-in you have 'won'. According to the books you 'win' a throw-in. And you look to throw it one way. No good. You go for another option. There aren't any. And the crowd is yelling 'Get on with it, book him ref . . .' and the referee is whistling, so you throw a fifty-fifty ball. And you lose it. That is the first time. Second time you get exactly the same thing. And then it gets to you. You think 'Oh, for pity's sake . . .' And that is the way games are won and lost. That is the way it is. Multiply that by fifty and that is what Leeds have done.

Again, Jackie Charlton goes up and stands in front of the goalkeeper for corners. Now you need your goalkeeper – he is crucial at corners. But he can't see the ball. Jack Charlton is standing in front of him. So straight away you are handicapped. Then he starts jumping up and down on the line. Pushes the full back. Pushes the centre half.

The first time you may get it away. The goalie somehow will get a desperate fist to it. But after about six corners, the keeper is thinking 'This fellow is driving me mad.' And he will stop. He won't go for the next ball. And Allan Clarke comes up and puts it in the net. So Leeds are 1–0 up. And why? Because Jackie Charlton has been driving people mad on the goal-line. That is football the way those people want to play it. You cannot beat them. You have to join them.

Les O'Neill is like that. After half an hour you are saying 'Oh no, not him again.' He is a pest. You get the ball and his leg sneaks through and knocks it away. That's all right the first time. But after about twenty minutes you cannot get on the ball. Every time you do, there is this pest pestering you. Driving you mad. And if you have got eleven fellows doing that to the other team you can stop them doing anything in the end. Because what happens then is that when you have the ball, the other guy thinks 'Here is my chance to get away from this pest' and he goes off and leaves you. You are a midfield player and you are marking a skilful player in the opposition. Right up his backside all the time. He can't find any space and he is sick of you. So your team gets the ball. And you run and take up a position. So he thinks 'I'm not going after him. If it breaks down and I go out here I might get the ball in space for once.' But what happens is that you now have space and so you can go on.

That is how games are won and lost in English football. More so at the lower level. But Leeds have developed that into an art. Nobody outside the game knows what it is like. It is like some fellow running up to your desk or work bench all day and sticking a pin in you then running away. The cumulative effect is drastic. By the second half you have had it with Jackie Charlton. You don't want to see him ever again. Norman Hunter is down the other end. Every time you get the ball – bang. He comes crashing in. That is the way they do it. Leeds, when they have got the ball, can play. Brilliantly. But they felt that was how they destroyed teams. Not by football. But by that. They played football once they had destroyed them.

Given how close English football is – how little difference there is between most sides – doing all these little things tips the balance in your favour. You drive them mad.

And that is what Carlisle have. I can see them driving people mad. Sheffield Wednesday, for example. A much better side on paper. But you would only have to do that to Craig for ten minutes.

But that is also the trouble with English football. Everyone is doing it. I've been doing it, and I'm meant to be a little ball-player. And that shouldn't be necessary. You have to have an element of it. But to be a good side you have also got to be able to play. It isn't necessary for everyone to be doing that. And the real problem, from what I have seen in the last couple of games, is the way it affects the good players.

They start trying to be even more intricate than they were before. If you have the ball and you want to lay off a simple ball, whatever the other bloke is trying to do shouldn't bother you. It bothers you when you are trying to do a little bit on the ball. Something a bit creative.

But what I've seen suggests that simplicity and creativity are often much nearer to being the same thing than we think. Simplicity is creativity a lot of the time. When you are being driven mad by someone you tend to start trying to squeeze things through gaps that don't exist; trying to produce the killer punch once and for all. He drives you crazy, and in the end the whole thing becomes crazy. Whereas if you are calm and try and play simple football, you still can.

Not every side does it for one thing. In the two games I've watched, Wednesday and Forest haven't done it to any great extent. But everyone is conditioned to it. So that even though it wasn't happening, people were expecting it and reacting as if it was. As soon as you put your toe on the ball you are expecting someone right up your ass. Because a lot of the Second Division is like that. You don't have time. So in the end you become a side who doesn't have time, because you won't give yourselves time. It is all part of the Second Division syndrome.

In the Second Division you do have less time than in the First. In the Third you have even less. What that means is that when you've got the ball some fool will come charging at you to put you under pressure. In the First they know they can't charge at Bobby Charlton, Johnny Giles or Billy Bremner. They will do you, because they are very very good. But in the Second Joe Bloggs gets it. And they think 'Well, if we go at him and dive in, he'll give us the ball a lot of the time.' And that is why they do it. But if Joe Bloggs begins to learn that the guy diving in can be beaten . . .

But that is the thing about the Second Division. Nobody ever seems to learn. Everyone accepts the game in the diver-in's context. That is what has happened to the game at the moment, and that is why it is so poor. People have settled for this lower level where kick and rush and bite and fight are the order of the day. No one has been brave enough to say 'No. We are not getting involved in that.'

4 Passing through the Slough of Despond?

8 October

I met Benny on the stairs this morning at the ground. 'Look after yourself,' he said. 'You'll be playing on Wednesday.'

I'd had a feeling that I would be back, because they had lost a couple of games, and Franky had been sent off. Although he will be eligible for the next two games, I had a feeling that Benny isn't happy with him in the side. I don't know why. He's a good honest pro, but somehow Benny doesn't rate him. That can happen with players. Managers can get these ideas, and then you've no chance. So his being sent off and having a suspension ahead gave Benny a good excuse to drop him. So I knew inwardly that I would be coming back in.

The 3–0 defeat by Forest was such a bad performance, especially the second half. I spent the second half sitting on the bench with Benny, Jack Blackman and Frank. It was obvious that things were coming to a head. Brownie is really struggling. I think he'll go; and Harry may go too, because we have got two good youngsters in the reserves just waiting. Listening to what Benny was saying about certain players, it was obvious that he is at the end of his tether with some of them. So there will be changes this week.

I had another chat with Kingy today. He is still desperate to get away. With all the press speculation about City and Arsenal being after him, he feels this is his chance, and if he can't take it he'll end up drawing his old-age pension at Millwall. He asked me what the best way of getting the transfer is. He is seeing Purser this week. I suggested again that he should try and extract a public commitment that he would be sold providing we were safe at Christmas. Of course no one would suggest that they were likely to go back on their word, but if they did they would be doing so publicly. So Kingy said that's what he will do.

9 October

There weren't that many changes. Robin Wainwright and Frank were dropped; Gordon Hill and I returned. Which meant a switch from 4–4–2 to 4–3–3; Denny and I have Gordon Bolland playing with us in midfield, but it looks as if Benny's new tactical development of midfield strikers has gone out of the window. And Brownie is still in.

We went to Deptford Park this morning. Normally Tuesday is our hard day. But while we are playing two matches a week you never really get down to it during the week.

But that doesn't disguise the fact that we aren't training right. Benny isn't getting out and getting things going at all. We need him organizing things, providing some sort of leadership. But at the moment he is not even coming out with us all the time. He seems curiously lacking in enthusiasm himself. So we go out to Deptford, and get on the Redgra feeling a bit fed up.

We started at half past ten. About 11.15 Benny turned up in his car, and came across and stood on the outside watching. Wearing his suit. He didn't say anything. Just stood on the outside watching. Whereas he should be inside, making it happen, providing some stimulation. But he was just a bystander, and all of a sudden he had gone.

I wondered what he is up to. He is supposed to have hurt his back. But that would not stop him coming out if he wanted to. One of his great assets has always been that he loves to come out to the training ground with the lads. Now he doesn't seem eager.

11 October

Millwall 0   Nottingham Forest 0

It was a nothing game really. They were a very unambitious side. No flair, nothing positive about them.

I think we can get a result up there in the replay. The League result last Saturday was a false one. Until Franky was sent off they had not wanted to know. They had got a lucky goal with their one shot. Apart from that they had tried nothing, had no ambition. They were dishonest really as a side. One or two of their players started really flashing after we were reduced to ten men, and Dennis said to their McKenzie as they were coming off 'See you on Wednesday at the Den. We'll see if you want to run so much there.' And they didn't. They did not want to run.

So although we only drew we weren't too worried about it. The general feeling was that we could get a result up there. It was not the normal optimism. It was a definite feeling that they were not a very good side, in spite of their position in the League. They are second or third, which gives an idea how false positions can be at this time.

Before the game Mickey Purser came into the dressing-room with his regular line: 'This is the one, my sons.' He always comes in around an hour beforehand when we are sitting around reading programmes and just starting to get changed. Always with his trilby in his hand, and always the same line. 'This is the one' with his fist clenched. We could be playing Oxford United on the last day of the season with nothing at stake, and he still comes in and says 'This is the one' and clenches his fist. I suppose he thinks he is doing his bit. I always think 'You're telling me? We need you to tell us that this is the one?' It's all so pointless, this idea of directors showing their faces. Another director, Burnige, always comes in too and wishes us the best, and Bill Nelan comes and cracks some jokes half an hour beforehand. But before a game you have left the world of directors and wives and kids and friends. You are in another world, tuned in on another wavelength.

Harold Wilson came in once. We were playing Huddersfield at the Den. No one was interested. I've got a fair interest in politics, but I can distinctly remember thinking 'Hurry up. It's getting a bit near, it's ten past two. See you later if you want to see us.' And if even the Prime Minister in the dressing-room, something which should have a real sense of occasion about it, means nothing, then the directors seem totally irrelevant.

Rickard never comes in. He is our '£5 at Christmas' man. He always gives it to us in an envelope. He gives it to the captain on the last away game before Christmas. The lads would be saying all the trip 'Well, where is it?' and suggesting that with inflation it should go up to a tenner. The idea that you give people earning £5,000 a year a fiver in an envelope doesn't appeal to me, to say the least. I don't think it really appeals to most of the lads. We use it to have a bet with or something. But it is typical of an attitude that is all too prevalent in football. This attitude of subservience. Directors are professional people in other spheres; we are professionals too. We should be respected as people, as equals. But all too often we aren't. Football smacks time and time again of the idea that somehow you aren't equal socially. Even benevolent directors are patronizing.

Which is one good thing about Millwall. No one there is pompous. It's a homely club.

12 October

The Irish team are having a training session at Bisham Abbey next week. John Giles has become manager now, and has recalled me to the squad after a two-year absence. Which is great. But when I went to see Benny today for permission to go he really hummed and hawed. He was really reluctant to let me go. He kept raising objections because we have this League Cup replay against Forest next Wednesday. Ireland are playing Poland on the following Sunday. He probably won't let me go, because we've got matches on the Saturday and Monday, but there's no reason why I shouldn't go to the training session except him being bloody-minded.

13 October

Millwall 0   Bristol City 2

It would be the 13th. Today was terrible. First off, there was trouble about the Irish squad. When they published the list in this morning's papers, my name was not in it. Millwall had not written back to tell the Irish FA that I was available, so they left my name off the list. I did not know what was happening. I wanted Benny to phone for me, but he wouldn't. In the end Gordon Borland, the club secretary, had a go. But as it was Saturday, there was no one at the Irish FA. So I had to try and track down John Giles. Leeds were away at Leicester, so in the end I had to leave a message for him at Leeds, and hope he would go back to their ground on his way home.

Then we went out to play Bristol. The thing about our side, the side which has played more or less consistently since the start of the season, is that it is already knackered. Knackered after seven or eight weeks. We are a tired, depressed side with low morale. The first time anything goes against you, you accept it.

We had always been a side which reacted very positively to a setback. The countless times we have been down, away from home, and come back to get a result! But not now.

Here we were against Bristol City. A useful side. Again the pitch was terrible. A dry, hard, firm pitch, and a windy day. It is the same for both teams, but the home side is always expected to do something, to be positive. And the away side's function is to defend. So the bad pitch suits the away side because all they have to do is get the ball away. They don't have to create so much. The home side has to get goals, create chances. They have to do the difficult creative things on the ball. You have to have a lot of movement, string your passes together, because invariably you get a lot more possession than the away team. So overall it suits the away team to play on a bad surface. Again, though, that comes down to morale. If your morale is high, you won't be so quick to blame the pitch. After ten minutes against Bristol, we were all saying 'Christ, how can you play on this bloody pitch!' After you had made one mistake you looked for an out.

We made a couple of chances in the first half, but basically they were holding us pretty well. And their morale is high. They are a young side: keen, ambitious, positive. They were tackling much more positively, quicker on to loose balls, and they threatened us a lot. But we went in o–o at half-time.

And we still felt we could get something. But it is a funny thing at the Den. We always kick a certain way in the first half, and the other way into our favourite end in the second. So in the event that we have to stage a rally, we are well set up.

This was the first time for months that we ended up playing the other way. I was worried about that as soon as we kicked off. If we are not in front by half-time we could be in trouble. The other end is a bit bleak, there is no atmosphere, and it doesn't inspire you. It is funny how important that is. If I were a manager, I would always try to find out which way the home side liked to kick, and try to frustrate them. When we came out for the second half, our task was that much harder because of it.

We disintegrated. They scored early on, and then really dominated the game, while we got worse and worse. By the end things were so bad it was a joke. At the end of the game I really thought relegation was a possibility. At least, a relegation battle. I don't think we would ever get relegated, because we have got character in the side. I don't think a side with character ever goes down. I know that is a great generalization, but I think on the whole it is a valid one.

The supporters really gave us some stick. Really vicious. I was walking off the pitch when I caught the eye of this big fat guy who stands just beside the tunnel. He goes to reserve games, everything. I've seen him all over the country. He seems really aggressive. I've never spoken to him, but I don't like him. I caught his eye, and he gave me the old wanking sign. Contempt. But there was not just contempt in his face, there was aggression also. And another guy sitting in the plastic seats under the stand said 'Why don't you go and work in a bar, because you can't bloody well play football?' He was just a respectable middle-aged guy with his kid, but he was really angry. This was about two or three minutes from the end when I was over there taking a throw-in. And at the end he came on to the pitch. I walked past quite close to him. I was going to have a go, say something, but I just kept walking. Still, it was really bad. Really made you wonder. Two home defeats on the trot in the League. Carlisle and now this.

Alan is getting married tomorrow. So it was a bad wedding present for him. He was really depressed. He's like me, he really takes the game seriously, and it does affect your home life. He doesn't come into the club and say 'I can't sleep because I'm so worried about our position' or tell you he's having rows with Sheila because worry is making him irritable. You don't do that. You hide everything. It's a funny thing about football. You live in really close proximity with people at work. You are much more dependent on them than people are on their workmates in most situations, but you never really reveal much to them.

But Alan does worry. He's a quiet, shy lad until you get to know him. But really strong. He always takes responsibility on the field, he'll really fight in tough situations. A great player. He doesn't catch the eye as much as someone who can trap the ball on his thigh, lob it over the defender's head and volley home, but he's equally important. He's got the ability to read a dangerous situation before it happens, and then go in and prevent it.

He and I have become very good friends. It took a long time, because he is quite shy. He's always gentle, not a bit aggressive. He is a real

competitor, but he channels it all into games – football, golf, even
Monopoly, Cluedo, cards. We generally spend an evening a week together
as a foursome, and most times we spend the evening playing games. We
always have a side bet on the game – Monopoly or whatever. And Alan
really plays to win. But he is tolerant along with his competitiveness. He
never runs anybody down. When I start holding forth about someone,
'Look what that bastard did today', he'll always say 'He's not a bad lad
though. He's got his good points', defending some of the people that are
landing us in the shit, and keeping people like Alan and Kitch, who are
really great players, and good, brave men, from the First Division football
they deserve.

So I was really delighted when he asked me to be his best man. We
went out this evening for his stag night. We went into Dockland, and
nobody had a go at us at any of the various places. Generally when they
recognized us and came up and talked, they had a go at Harry and
Brownie. People were saying 'Those two have got to go', that sort of thing.
And you can't comment. You can't agree or disagree. You just have to
shrug your shoulders and smile.

But I still didn't know about the Irish trip. John Giles called me, and
said I was included, so that is all right. But I didn't ask Benny whether I
could go or not. I thought that if he had been unhappy about it on Friday,
he'd be even more unhappy after today's shambles. So I shall corner him
at the wedding when he's got a few scotches inside him and feeling
benevolent.

14 October

Alan's wedding went off very well. It was strange seeing all the players
with their wives, and dressed up in their best. We don't socialize much as
a group. People live so far apart, and London is such a big place. Alan
and I see a lot of one another. Dennis and Harry are good friends, and
some of the young lads probably drink together, but generally we do not
socialize much. So it was strange seeing them all here, and Benny and his
wife. And Jack Blackman out of his tracksuit. He is amazing. He is about
sixty, always at the club first, always the last to leave, and always in a
tracksuit. I did not recognize him in a suit.

Yesterday's failure was all more or less forgotten. Players don't carry it over to their social life. They are very resilient. You compensate for failure by saying 'Damn it. We're alive, we're getting a good living, and there is simply no use worrying about it.' Now our situation after yesterday was so desperate and disappointing. We had lost all belief in the club, and in ourselves as a group. You always believe in yourself; but in ourselves as a group, our faith was tarnished. You look at everything and you say 'He's got to go. He is not doing it. Nor is he. Nor is he.' But you never lose belief in yourself. The last person a player looks at is himself. He'll look at his colleagues, the manager, the crowd and the club. The last person he will look at is himself.

Take Brownie. He has been having a terrible time. He has let himself get overweight. He has got a lot of talent, and he has had a good run in the first team for four or five years. He has already had a free transfer from Chelsea, so he knows the feeling of failure. Which should have whetted his appetite for success, and for security. Yet it has not.

He is only twenty-two or twenty-three, he has not been playing well, and he knows there is this good youngster waiting to take his place. But he refuses to recognize it. He is as happy-go-lucky after the game as anyone, and he has probably had the worst time of anyone. He will blame anyone rather than look at himself. We all would, but some of us can recognize the dangers.

Gordon Bolland has been having a bad time, as we all have. But Gordon recognizes it, and is worried, really worried, about it. He is desperate to try and change it. Which is why Gordon has been in the game fourteen or fifteen years, has had a good career and will go on having one. Whereas Brownie might struggle, because of a crucial difference in attitude.

Benny did not seem particularly happy, but he agreed to let me go to Bisham Abbey. So of course I began to worry that meant he was planning to drop me. But there was nothing I could do about that. I really wanted to be back in the Irish squad, so I came on to Bisham after the wedding, in spite of my fears.

When I got to Marlow three of the lads, Paddy Mulligan, Joe Kinnear and Ray Treacy, were waiting at the station to pick me up. We drove back to Bisham and met John Giles. I had really missed being part of the Irish team. It was really good to meet people again.

15 October

When you get footballers away from their normal environment like this, there is a marvellous sense of freedom. Whether it is on tour or at an international training camp doesn't matter. You are away from your normal routine and with new people, or people you haven't seen for a while. There is a great freshness.

At the Irish team meetings, you never know who is going to be there. Every time it is a new set of faces. They keep finding English players with Irish grandmothers or great-aunts. Terry Mancini is here this time. A most unlikely Irishman! But the great thing about football is that someone like that, whom you have never met before, is there, and immediately you get on. There may be ten of you in a room who have never met before, but you sit down and have a cup of tea, and already there is a tremendous feeling of comradeship. You identify with one another immediately.

You can have sixteen lads from sixteen different clubs. Some are successful, some aren't. But the things that happen to you are so common, footballers always have something to talk about.

It can be very reassuring too. Because you always feel your club and its problems are unique, that things happen there that wouldn't happen at successful clubs. And you think that is why they are successful, while your club isn't. But it is not so. Because every footballer will tell you the same stories about the managers and the coaches. And one thing you learn is that the image is never the man.

This came out strongly at tea. I was sitting with Paddy Mulligan and John Giles. Paddy was saying 'We haven't seen Allison for three months.' And we all thought he was working on the pitch with the players every day!

At the other extreme there was Leeds. Coaching came up, as it always does in these get-togethers. We had this discussion last night about coaches and what they try to do. We were talking about the daft team talks they give, and the daft phrases they use. I was telling them about Lawrie, and John said 'Yes, but Les is similar at Leeds. The boss has to allow him to talk at the end of our team talks. He always asks "Got anything to say, Les?" and Les will drone on for five minutes. It's never very relevant, though.' So Les Cocker, this great figure as we see him, is seen as irrelevant by the Leeds lads in the same way as we see Lawrie.

John was also moaning about the coaching the young lads got at Leeds. He, Bremner and Allan Clarke had enough power to ignore all the bad technical advice they were given, but the young lads didn't.

We all agreed that coaching has got completely out of hand. So many people are going around with techniques, functions and conditioned games. Some of the conditioned games you hear about are incredible. Among the ones the lads produced were: having to go round the back of the goal and square it back before you could score; having to pass it backwards before you could score; and a one-touch finish.

So you find out that although you thought it was only your coach at your club, it really is the same for everyone. It's a good scale to measure your own club against, and to measure the values in the game. You always tend to think that if your club is not doing well, it is because they have all the wrong values and do all the wrong things. So what is the mystery? John says they don't train hard at Leeds once the season starts, because they have two games a week. So they spend most of the time playing five-a-sides. Yet some clubs have you climbing mountains all the week.

At Palace they take vitamin pills. At tea Paddy pulled all these pills and capsules out and started popping them in his mouth.

'What's all this, then?'

'Vitamins. It's what we have to do.'

'Do you feel any better for it?'

'No, not really. No different.'

Paddy was also telling us about their psychologist and his current theory that you pass more often to your friends. Of course, that brought everyone diving in with cracks. 'Do you all hate each other at Palace, then?', 'Got a lot of great friends in the opposition then, Paddy?', that kind of thing.

Paddy, John, Ray Treacy and I had a fascinating discussion this evening about what is the prime motivating factor in football. John said it was fear. I thought pride. In numbers I lost hands down 3-1.

It is interesting watching John, and listening to his theories. I was very impressed with the way he intends to manage. Of course he hasn't really been subjected to the strains yet, and the real test is how your theories stand up under pressure. But I'm very impressed with him so far. I think he will be a major force in the game in years to come. He knows the game. He is very good at handling people, and he is a very attractive character. Not a bit pompous, but he commands respect immediately. He'll do very well.

Tomorrow I've got to leave early to get the train up to Forest for the League Cup replay. It has been playing on my mind a bit. I went to bed for a rest this afternoon, but I'm worried I shall be dropped again after the last couple of bad results.

17 October

Nottingham Forest 1   Millwall 3

When I got back to London from Marlow to go up to Nottingham, I had just missed the team train. So had Gordon Bolland, so we went up together. He was worried too. He felt he was going to be dropped. It was very strange. We did this three-hour train journey together, and it was either him or me who was going to be dropped.

We are good friends really. We have spent six or seven years together, and we have always been quite close. He is a genuine good professional. I did not think Benny would drop Gordon. Because Gordon scores goals. But Gordon told me Brownie was dropped, Harry was dropped, and Stevie Brown was in the team. Brownie I had expected to be dropped. But he was right off the sheet, which is unusual. Normally when you are dropped, you stay on the sheet as twelfth or thirteenth man.

Gordon also said 'We are playing 4–2–4.' Which was also news. 'So it looks like you or me, Eamon. And I think it will be me. I'm pretty sure it is me.'

But there wasn't any awkwardness. We are both professionals and good friends.

This morning the news of Clough being fired (or resigning) had appeared, and we met this lady journalist on the train going to interview Clough's wife. No appointment or anything. A foot-in-the-door job. We felt sorry for her.

When we got there we went to the Midland Hotel in Derby to join the team for lunch. The table I was on also had Harry, Alf, Dennis, Benny, Mr Rickard, Kitch and Alan. And we started talking about Clough.

It was an interesting discussion in that it mirrored attitudes perfectly.

You really raise the temperature when you start talking about Clough. Players like him very much. He says the things we all feel, he hits the right targets. I think most professionals have this same sympathy for him. Personally I think he is too blunt, and that there is not enough dignity in what he is doing. But it is nice to see someone who has made it not selling out.

Directors hate him. He is too much for them to cope with. Mr Rickard said he was only a cheque-book manager. Which is crazy. He is anything but that.

Then Benny launched into this long tirade. Not exactly a defence of the Derby board, but saying how arrogant Clough was, and how bad for the game people like Clough and Allison were. He said they demean it. Although they are successful, they have got too much to say for themselves. We had this discussion about Clough's merits, which was futile. Dennis would not discuss it. Because when Benny starts like that, you cannot say anything. He just talks, and won't let anyone get a word in. He always tells me I don't listen to anyone, but he is the last person to listen in a situation like that. He got quite heated. It must bother him a lot. He likes to think of everyone doing their job quietly and efficiently without making waves. He cannot understand why someone like Clough wants to attack all those guys like Hardaker.

After lunch we went to bed for a rest before the game. I still did not know if I was playing. After our rest we went to Nottingham. When we were in the changing-room, Benny called me outside. And that is the kiss of death. The crooked finger. I went out feeling totally resigned to it. I just walked out after him and said 'Come on, surprise me.'

So he said 'How do you feel?'

I had been away from the squad, and they always think you debauch yourself on these occasions. Sometimes that is true, sometimes not. This time not. No way at Bisham Abbey. The nearest we came was a gay waiter. And he was already taken when I got there!

So I said 'Yeah, I feel great. Great!' No way I'm giving him the opportunity of dropping me on the pretext I'm not fit.

So he looked at me and said 'OK, OK, I believe you. Good. I'll leave Gordon on the bench tonight then.'

I went back into the dressing-room first. The lads looked up expectantly, but I had this large grin on my face. So they all thought 'Well . . .'

Then Benny came in and went straight over to Gordon and told him.

Harry and Brownie had been dropped, so we were going to play these two young full backs that Benny had got on free transfers from Arsenal and Spurs – Dave Donaldson and Eddie Jones. They are very good players. Very young, very talented.

We had Stevie Brown wide on the right wing, and Gordon Hill wide on the left, with Dennis and me in midfield. So we were playing 4–2–4, which is really revolutionary stuff in the Second Division away from home.

The atmosphere was incredible. A kind of 'What the hell, we can't get any lower than Saturday.' So the pressures were off. It was a release, and we were trying something different. And something I don't think any of us really expected to succeed. So that if we failed we had this let-out. We could all say 'Fancy playing 4–2–4 away from home with four youngsters. Crazy!'

I knew the young full backs would do well, but I was worried about the two whizz-kids on the wing. Two kids with talent. But they are not Johnny Giles, either of them. And in the Second Division talent is not necessarily the prime source of results.

But it was really good. Hard work for Dennis and me in the middle of the park. When there are only two of you, instead of sometimes four, and nearly always three, it is a bit of a job. They pressed us early on, but they were very unwilling. And we knocked it about with a kind of gay abandon. Playing one-twos, little flicks here, little flicks there. Most un-Second Division. Not the normal tight, grim, unrewarding hard graft. Instead it was strolling around, knocking it about. The pitch was great. And the kids were really playing well, all of them.

The full backs were quick in the tackle, composed under pressure. As the game progressed, we really started to express ourselves. You don't often get that in the Second Division, the fear factor is too great. You usually get players limiting themselves to the minimum amount of flourish, and playing the safe straight moves.

We had one or two hairy moments when we were a bit thin at the back, and a red horde threatened us, but we survived. Fortune favouring the brave, I suppose. And ten minutes before half-time we got a good goal.

I felt a kind of wry amusement at the whole situation. Here we were with four very young players on the extreme flanks, knocking the ball around with not a care in the world. And all of a sudden we get this goal. So we went in 1–0 up at half-time.

Great. Everyone was happy. Confidence had surged back in. But at the same time the pressure was back on again, because we had something to defend again. Something to lose.

And then we were lucky. Because we got a second goal and then a third very quickly. Both the result of their defensive mistakes. And so we were 3–0 up with twenty minutes to go.

And then at that stage I got really worried for some reason. My bottle went. I suppose because I could suddenly see a victory I had not really expected. I started looking at the clock and wondering 'Could they get four goals in twenty minutes? Or can they get three, because if it goes to extra time, that is it. We will be too knackered.'

We kept playing attractive football. They were desperate, and pushed a couple more forward. And eleven minutes from time they got one. I started screaming at people. I was really panicking. Swindon again, in a way; but it would have been worse this time round because we had all these young lads. If they had made it 3–2 it would have been really difficult. And this crazy referee gave them an indirect free kick inside the box because someone shouted at him. But they didn't score. We took a bit of pressure in the last ten minutes but we managed it all right. We survived 3–1.

It was fantastic afterwards. All these young lads, Stevie coming back after a long time, and two making their debuts, and we had got this great result. We could not quite believe it. You do not expect to play 4–2–4 and win Cup games away from home like that.

And we have got a home draw in the next round. We are thinking of the League Cup now as a compensation for having failed in the League. Two from the bottom we are. We have got no chance. But last night we were perfectly happy. If you had asked us six weeks earlier how we would feel if we were third from bottom and had lost our last two home games, but on the other hand were in the third round of the League Cup, we would have said 'Terrible'. But we didn't. We felt all right. Because a week is a long time in football. A day is a long time in football. The last result, that is all. If Palace win on Saturday they will feel great. Now if you had asked them at the beginning of the season how they would feel if they were seven points adrift at the bottom and they won a game making it five points adrift, they would have been speechless. Probably not able to envisage how awful they would feel. But if they win on Saturday, they will feel great. One win and you are away. The dream is on again and off you go.

The two young full backs did really well. After the game it was clear that they are in the side for keeps. You could see them still there in five or six years' time. They were that impressive. Which means Benny has pulled off another coup. Two players for nothing. Both must be worth £50,000 now. And people in the game are saying 'You can't find players.' Managers are going into the transfer market spending fortunes. Allison wanted to pay Oldham £70,000 for a full back. I guarantee he is no better than these two lads. Benny does really well.

It proves also that there are players around, players who have not made it with big clubs. I'd love to know why. Something obviously went wrong for these lads at big clubs. Something obviously destroyed that delicate thing called confidence. Of course they are very different. Eddie is a quiet, determined character. David is a bit flash, a bit arrogant. He likes to have a bit of fun. The sort of lad you have always got to keep an eye on, to make sure he keeps at it.

It makes you wonder what went wrong for them at Arsenal and Spurs. I mean, those two lads failed. They got kicked out of Spurs and Arsenal. In April, when they were given free transfers, the bottom fell out of their world. But they have retained their belief in themselves, and the ambition and the desire to succeed. And they came to our club. From being just a number, they have become recognized individuals. It is a small staff, and you feel you are a person. Whereas at a big club with maybe forty pros, you can become lost. And that can have a dramatic effect.

When you are young, you think you are important. You think you have some worth as a player and as a person. But when there are forty other guys around the place, the coaches and the manager can easily ignore you.

And if you are ignored in that way it can be destructive. Young players constantly need to be boosted.

These two lads are going to be in the side for a long time to come. Therefore Harry is finished at Millwall as a player. Very very sad. He is the greatest professional I have ever played with. Probably the greatest Millwall ever had. A legend, and rightly so. It is very sad to see. He still comes away with us now. But if the day should come when he is left right off the sheet there will be an incredible sense of loss. I think everyone will miss him.

But my first thought afterwards was of Brownie. Because he was not even in the party. The lads were saying 'He'll hang himself when he hears this result.' I felt for him. Because these lads played so well, in my opinion he is going to struggle at Millwall. For the last few months he has been downhill all the way. A sad waste of talent.

18 October

John Giles has picked me for the Irish team, but Benny refuses to release me. We have games on Saturday and Monday; Ireland are playing Poland in Dublin on Sunday.

Everyone at the club is happy, though. That win at Forest has done wonders. Maybe the older players don't really believe it, but the young lads are really flying. Stevie in particular. He has had a long spell of feeling down. Now he is back and full of beans. A lot of chat, high spirits.

Benny is very brave playing 4–2–4. Maybe it will work, but it means a lot depends on Dennis; there is only he and I in midfield. And I'm still not convinced about him. He has wanted to pick the team before, not really tried when Stevie has been in because he doesn't rate him. And now there are two inexperienced young wingers with a lot to learn. Either could turn Dennis off by doing something silly.

We'll see what happens at Bolton on Saturday. They haven't started well, feeling their way a bit in the higher Division, but they are a good young side. If we nick something there, it will be an achievement.

I had a little session with Benny today. There was I sitting innocently enjoying my post-training cup of tea, when Benny came up and gave me the evil eye to come into the office.

'What's all this rubbish about public commitment you've been filling Kingy's head with?'

I launched into a detailed explanation of how I was thinking that the lad's best interests and our best interests were the same; that players desperate to get away were disruptive, etc., but there was no way he'd buy that one. It was a fair cop. Kingy had cracked under pressure and said I'd suggested that approach. Benny said 'Well, I didn't think he would think of that one on his own.'

Oh well, that's me back in the role of villain again.

19 October

Our five-a-sides are a joke at the moment. Everyone is messing around pleasing themselves. The whole thing is completely out of hand. We are all going our own way, doing our own thing.

Stevie is magic in them, though. He is always picked very early because he always takes an interest. He proves what a good player he is in five-a-sides. He seems to spend it all during the week, and has nothing left by the time Saturday comes round. If anyone saw him during the week they would think he was worth £200,000. It is interesting how some players are brilliant in five-a-sides and can't do it on Saturday. And sometimes you see the opposite.

Another interesting thing is how someone who is just about to strike form in the first team on Saturday will always start off by doing well in the five-a-sides. And conversely the fellow who is having a bad time in the first team will have a bad time in them too. Always clumsy and just that shade off the mark in timing and confidence.

Picking teams for five-a-sides is interesting. You never get the eleven first-teamers as the first picks. A lot of people go for the dependable type of player, so you get a good dependable reserve player picked very early. Billy Neill is always one of the first to be picked even now he is finished as a player. I've always been one of the last, even when I've been having a great time in the first team. What you look for is someone who will steam around the place getting the ball, then giving it to YOU. It's great when it is fun, but we get a lot of fighting in five-a-sides.

In many ways five-a-sides are more part of your life than Saturdays. Because you spend five days training, and only one day is Saturday. So what happens during the week is crucial to what happens on Saturday.

The trouble at the moment is that we are playing two games just about every week. So there is no chance to work on the game much in midweek. Whether we would anyway is questionable, but it is difficult to sort things out when we are committed to two games a week the whole time.

21 October

Bolton Wanderers 0   Millwall 1

Our best game of the season. We defended really well against a good young side. They are inexperienced, but very keen. The complete opposite of Forest. They wanted to win. They were keen, bright and aggressive. And we had to battle.

The two kids at full back did great again. And of course we have got Gordon Hill in the side now. The lad we have christened Merlin the Magician. An incredible kid. He is only seventeen, but he's got incredible self-confidence. He has taken some unmerciful stick from the lads – from no one more so than me. And he just bounces back. You cannot insult him.

He is maddening to play with. I like players whose play I can predict, players who you can play with, as opposed to players who are doing their own thing all the time. And he is definitely doing his own thing all the time. He has learnt a little, but I doubt his capacity to learn much. And without the capacity to learn at seventeen, there is no way you can make it.

But if you try and instil too much common sense into him, you will destroy his capacity for the spontaneous, the unusual. Which is a considerable asset in his game. He turns full backs, he does unusual things on the ball, he creates unusual situations. Benny likes him, and we are probably wrong in our judgement of him. Professionals are not always the best judge of their fellows. We tend to like players who do straightforward things we can understand, so we know where we are. But if you get too much of that, you get a dull side. If eighty per cent of his game was constructive, and twenty per cent was turning full backs inside out and creating situations out of nothing, great. But at the moment the eighty per cent which should be constructive is nothing.

He gives the ball away. And the ball is precious in football. It's the whole thing. You get the ball and keep it. Keep it until something is on. You hate to see anyone giving it away. And at the moment his game is eighty per cent giving it away, and only twenty per cent creative. Which is the wrong balance.

Also he is not very good at picking people up. And in a situation like yesterday you need all eleven working. When you say to him 'Watch that full back', he just watches him race away. He literally just watches him.

We have not been too hard on him out on the park. I've had a couple of goes at him, but basically we have just suffered in silence. He has scored a goal or two, and created some good situations. Maybe Benny can see the whole situation better in the stand than we can on the pitch. But I would rather see Dougy in the side because I think he both creates situations and is constructive. And he is a willing learner.

But Gordon made the winning goal yesterday, after we had absorbed all this pressure. He had not been doing very well. When we were walking out for the second half he said to me 'I love these tops.' It was greasy on top.

I was tempted to say 'You wouldn't have thought so, the way you performed first half', but I didn't. I said 'Oh yeah?'

And then he made the winning goal. He is incredible.

Clarky has adopted him. They get the train together every day. They room together now on away trips. We've been kidding them they have got something on because they are always together. They make an odd pair. Clarky is a big burly thirty-two-year-old pro who has been around and Gordon is seventeen, five foot nothing, a wide-eyed kid. An extraordinary situation.

Benny has told us to leave him alone. Which is the worst thing he could have said. We had this team talk, and Benny told Gordon not to take any notice of anybody out on the park. Benny does not want us to destroy him by trying to tell him too much. He just wants Gordon to go out and do it. But it is the worst thing he could have said, because you get a situation like a free kick. And you tell Gordon to pick up the full back. And he looks at you as much as to say 'Benny has told me not to take any notice of you.' And meanwhile the full back is standing wide completely on his own.

And at corner kicks you say 'Pick him up! Gordon!' and he shrugs. You can see his mind working, thinking 'Benny's told me not to take any notice of that . . .' So he stands there. You scream at him. Then he goes and picks the bloke up. But he does it as much as to say 'I shouldn't really be doing this. The boss told you to leave me alone.'

Gordon used to be a very good-class amateur, and good amateurs tend to think there is nothing to the professional game. They think they can be as good as Bobby Charlton. Or, if not as good as Bobby Charlton, certainly as good as the run-of-the-mill professionals. Football is a joy for them, plus a tenner in the boot as a bonus. And you can be the local hero in Hitchin or Wycombe.

It's nice. No pressures. You have got your job and your family; so you can ponce around every Saturday, do a little bit, and you are a star. I don't like amateurs. They get up my nose. I know football as my living, as a hard life. A joyful life, but a very hard one. It is not a question of a tenner in the boot, it is my wife and child's livelihood. You are totally committed to football. Amateurs' lives are a bit luxurious compared to ours.

So when they come into professional football, their attitude is different to ours. When Gordon came here, he was incredible. He thought it was just a matter of time until he got into the first team. Not a question of when and if. Just when. And he was so young at the time, and there was no question of his getting into the first team. But then Dougy got injured and he was in all of a sudden.

I was in football for six years before I even got near a Football League match. I don't hold that against him. It's great, if you can do it. But he is like Alice in Wonderland at the moment. He is going out and turning these big burly full backs inside out. They are all trying to kick him, and they can't, and he has not got a care in the world. He goes out and does a few flicks, and it is great. He must think 'What is all this about it being hard to break into League football? I've done it in six weeks.' Which is great for him.

But you can't help laughing, because he has such a big shock to come. He has probably always thought there was nothing to this League football game. And everything that has happened to him so far has confirmed that opinion. He probably sees us stumbling all over the place, and thinks 'Hell, what has he got lines all over his face for? It's great, is this!' It's like a kid let loose in Woolworth's for a day. But the security guards will be after him soon.

A nice illustration of why his namesake is such a good referee. Gordon Hill is probably the referee players respect the most. We had him yesterday. I got caught in possession and whacked. And I was on the ground having treatment when he came over to see what was up. It was hurting, so I said 'Fucking hell, you let him get away with that.'

And he said 'Last year you wouldn't have been caught like that, you would have avoided it. You're fucking going, you are. Getting past it.'

I let him have another mouthful at that, but then I had to laugh. It hurt a bit, but it was a good response. It showed that he knew the game a little bit. And some referees book you for swearing at your own centre half. You can't take a liberty with him. You couldn't call him a f . . . . . . c . . . and get away with it. Which is right; but when you use industrial language as you are bound to and get booked it is ridiculous. A referee cost me £300 once. I got sent off at Burnley. I didn't tell the referee to 'fuck off', I just used the word. That is daft. Everyone says 'fuck'. If you draw the analogy between the football field and the trenches, which is a common analogy in the game, it is absurd to expect the man going over the top not to say it occasionally. And if you say 'For fuck's sake' to Gordon Hill, he will say 'Well, what is the fucking matter with you ?', which is fine because then you are operating on some kind of level. And at the same time he is probably the last referee you can take liberties with.

We had an amusing scene on the train coming home too. A whole gang of journalists coming home from the big game in Manchester came into the dining-car while we were there. Including this lady football writer. They were all giving her the big chat. One bought her dinner – one of the fat middle-aged hacks. The lads went spare. 'What is she doing with that fat slob?' 'Oh, she's not great herself.' 'She is a lot prettier than him, though.'

What was even funnier was that he got off at Watford, and one of the others dived in immediately.

Players have a double standard towards journalists. On the one hand they despise them, thinking they know nothing about the game. This comes out in particular when you've snatched a point away from home. A 1-1 draw away from home is fantastic. All the lads get in the bath saying 'Fantastic!' You ignore the fact that your keeper has performed ten miracles, the woodwork is worn out, and they have missed eight sitters. We had years of that sort of performance. And then you nick a goal in the eighty-ninth minute, in off their full back's head. You just simply ignore things like that. You have worked for it and you achieved it. Now you have got it, and no poncy newspaper reporter is going to take it away from you. You get in the bath afterwards with all the lads and it's 'Great.' And the manager is glowing and he is around you all the time saying 'Well done, lads, fantastic! That was a lot better' – than some other time when you played well and got done.

Then you get on the train, picking up the local paper at the station. And the paper says 'Numerous near misses', 'Dreary Millwall scrape last-minute draw', and the lads will go 'Bastard!' And you read the report saying 'Millwall, pinned in their own 18 yard box for 89 minutes, completely out-played, out-witted, and out-thought, managed to salvage a point with a lucky own goal in the 90th minute. This was a really fine performance by Hull (or Bolton or Cardiff or whoever), who played Millwall off the park.' And by this time the lads are frothing, and the carriage is strewn with torn-up newspaper. You are really cut up. 'What is the man talking about? It wasn't like that at all.'

We went one down, we had a lot of pressure, we absorbed it, we came back fighting, and we set ourselves this tremendous task. So the guy put it into his own net, but we pressured him into putting it there. That is our story.

On that level, the journalist's views have some validity. But on a deeper level they don't know what is going on on a pitch. All of them can do a straightforward match report. But they don't understand what they are seeing most of the time. They may see that Millwall won the midfield battle. But they don't know why. They have no idea that we were pushing up tight on them when they had possession, forcing them to go deeper, and stopping them playing, while they were giving us space to come further forward, and giving us room to turn and spray it about. You say that to a journalist, and he won't know what you are talking about. Whereas theatre critics and film critics do know what the mechanics of a production are, most football writers don't. So players tend to despise journalists.

On the other hand, players are flattered by their attention. Flattered by the idea that this guy has come along especially to write about them. So you have contempt and at the same time a slight awe at seeing your name in print. And players tend to have a special face that they show to journalists. Among ourselves we show a face that isn't really our true face. We show something less than what we really are. Being part of a group means you conform to group standards and keep other aspects hidden to some extent. Something a manager can't get away with. He is there to be seen and exposed to his players. They will know him within seven days. They will sort out his strengths and weaknesses immediately.

With a journalist a player shows another side to the one he shows his colleagues. Journalists and players have an uneasy relationship really. It doesn't work very well. Journalists always have their preconceptions, their angles. And they then tend to try and make the player say the things they want him to say. And it is all too easy for journalists to do this. They don't go into a story to discover but to substantiate preconceived ideas. This shows particularly when they are on the 'discontented player' story. They very rarely find the real cause of the discontent. Instead they encourage him to make a fool of himself and repeat all the old clichés. He will probably repeat them. But a little understanding and sensitivity would produce a better picture.

What is important in the game is how it is played. How people are motivated to do the bad things, and how they are motivated to do the good things. And what is going on at a club at a particular time. What stage the club is at in the process of success and failure. How a game went, or why something happened. You very rarely read that. They personalize that, and it becomes a game of personalities. And if there aren't enough personalities, they create them. And that is destructive.

23 October

Millwall 5   Preston North End 1

We always expect to win at home. Teams hate coming to the Den. Which is partly why we beat the Football League record for being undefeated at home. When I first went there I used to hate it. I remember going there with York City for my first visit. It took us half an hour to find the place. Eventually we went up this dingy back street. I remember thinking 'Where is this?' Then you go and have a look at the pitch, which is bumpy, terrible. And you think 'Oh Jesus, what are we doing here?' The dressing-rooms are terrible. Small poky places. The away team dressing-room is a dungeon, no light, no window. The bathrooms are horrible. Then you get out there to face them – the Lions. And they come storming at you and most sides jack it in.

When you have been there a little time, though, you grow to love it. You feel secure in it. It's one of our biggest assets.

Yesterday we played well right from the start. Stevie was doing well, doing his little bit, and we got one right away. And I thought 'Well, that is it! According to the script, they should fall apart.' They didn't, though. Not then. They kept playing their football. They are up at the top, so obviously they aren't going to swallow it as easily as a team that is half-way. So they kept going. And just before half-time they got this poxy goal. Which we thought was right out of the blue. Any time any team scores at the Den you think they have committed highway robbery. We went in at half-time sick about the goal. We have been struggling at the back all season. Things haven't been fitting into place. But we never expect to be punished. Especially at home.

Kingy is having a bad time for him. He is not coming off his line. And he is not shouting, which is a weakness in his game. He has not got many weaknesses, but that is one. He is not good at organizing things, telling people when to clear it and when not to, when it is his ball and when it is not. All of which he should. Defenders live off a good goalkeeper.

But then after a couple of minutes in the second half we went ahead. Their centre half boobed. He tried to knock it back to the goalkeeper, didn't make contact, Alfie nipped in and we were 2–1 up. So in our minds it was all over. We were attacking the Cold Blow Lane end. All of a sudden we started playing well, and they caved in. Their defenders started making mistakes. Stevie was doing great wide on the right, while Hilly was performing miracles on the left. We got another one. 3–1. Then it was a case of every man doing his party tricks. Indulging himself, flicking it here, flicking it there, beating a couple at a time, crossing it, having a shot. Taking it down on your thigh or your chest.

I hate all that. The one thing about English football is that you have forty-two battles, more or less. Battle is what the game is all about in the Second Division. And you come to have a taste for it, to enjoy it. And you tend to get turned off by something that is too easy. In the second half it was one burst of applause after another – bits of brilliance all over the place. And every time we shot it seemed to go into the net. It was all academic long before the end.

We played 4–2–4 again with Dennis and me in the middle of the park. Dennis had a real carefree air right from the start. It was as if he'd said to himself 'What have we got to lose?' and it all came off. But football just is not carefree. People were doing things they just are not capable of reproducing half the time, let alone all the time. I got much more satis-faction out of the Sheffield Wednesday game where we nicked it in the last minutes. That was a much truer reflection of what we would have to face in the season. The kind of game you have to win to do something. That is what is important: are you capable of winning the kind of battles you are going to face? Not: are you capable of stuffing a side which is already stuffed anyway?

The win, though, has put us right back in it. We're only six points behind Middlesbrough, who are top. And we have got them to come on Saturday. If we beat them we are right back in it. And obviously we expect to beat them at home.

But I'm not happy somehow. I don't think we have got the right side. I don't believe the theory that you should leave a winning team alone. If you have won with two of your best players out of the side, you should bring them back in. Because sooner or later you are going to have to bring them back in.

We have got four new lads in the side now. Two new young full backs, two new wingers. And Clarky too is new to the team. It worries me, because the side we had at the beginning of the season was a really good one. We had been together for a long time. I thought it would stand us in good stead as the season went on. Now we have got Dougy, Harry, Gordon and Brownie all out. And although we have done it for a couple of games without them, Dougy and Gordon and Harry are the kind of lads who will serve you in good stead. I don't know these new lads. I know Stevie and I know Hilly, and I don't really fancy them for the long trek ahead. And that worries me.

You see Gordon and Dougy out of things in training. Training with the reserves. Or in fact you don't see them a lot of time, because they are out when you are in and vice versa. Playing in the bloody Midweek League. And now we have got a hell of a chance getting back up there. We have recovered really from a bad start. We are in it again. It is coming together. But the basis is not there.

The other worrying thing is that the morale is still pretty rocky. The team spirit is good, we are all good friends. But there is something eating away underneath. There is this feeling that it is not quite right. I don't know what it is. I really can't analyse it, except that Benny seems so distant, so withdrawn. He seems apart from things in a way that he never has been before. Which is strange.

24 October

Everyone in the club was flying today after Monday night. Especially the kids. Three wins in a row: two away, then a big one at home. Everyone was bubbling. All the doubts have temporarily disappeared. Which is not the best of preparations for playing Middlesbrough. When you are playing a really good side on the Saturday, a big win in midweek can be the worst thing that can happen. Because it can lull you into a false sense of security. It softens you up.

We got one good laugh, though. Derek Smethurst has been picked in goal for this afternoon's reserve game. He has played there in five-a-sides, but this seems incredible. It looks as if Benny has finally decided to do something about us not having a reserve goalkeeper. We haven't had one for some time. They seem to rely on Kingy never getting injured – or on his bravery so that he is always willing to play when only seventy-five-percent fit.

25 October

When we were changing before training, Harry told me that Dennis had been up to Hull yesterday to talk terms. He apparently has not decided whether to go or not, because there is still some question about his money. Dennis did not say anything about it. But it sounds likely that he will move. Harry sounded envious.

It is an incredible situation. Here we are with a real chance of getting back into the race, and Dennis looks as if he is getting out.

It is a strange situation. On the one hand, maybe it is for the best. It has become clear that Dennis and Benny will never resolve their differences. You get the impression that Benny has been sitting brooding about what to do about Dennis rather than being out getting our problems sorted out on the training ground. In that sense, although we will miss him as a player, maybe it means we can concentrate on making better use of our resources.

On the other hand, who is going to play in his place and give us what he gives us? He gives us a bit of authority and experience, and a lot of skill. I shall miss him a lot. He helps me by winning the ball and doing the things I'm not very good at, but find myself having to do when he is missing. If they have got a hard man, Dennis will keep him occupied. But if Dennis is missing, then their ball winner will dominate the midfield physically. Because getting the ball is of major importance.

Certainly at the moment his contribution is a bit questionable, because he is disillusioned with the club. But I would rather see him disciplined and doing his stuff for us than replaced by somebody of lesser ability.

And it is also worrying in terms of where we are going. It tends to knock on the head the idea that we are ambitious and about to go somewhere. Why sell him now, of all times? If we were going to let him go, why not do it last season when we were half-way and clearly not going to make it? Then we would have had time to recover from it. Time to build. But now it will be Christmas before we adjust, and by then it will all be over. It is not as if it is a new problem, after all.

Dougy Allder is very depressed at the moment. I tried giving him a little gee in the five-a-side. 'Don't worry, Doug, you'll be back in a few weeks.' 'I'll never get back in, never.' It is a dangerous time, particularly if you are young. When the first team has won three on the trot, things seem hopeless. You despair, and the despair can easily turn into self-pity. You can let your spirit disintegrate, stop trying in reserve matches, take it easy in training and finally lose the will to fight back.

That seems to have happened to Brownie. He has not shown any real reaction to being dropped. He just seems bewildered. So distressed that he cannot react at all.

The young lads like Stevie and Ned Kelly have never had any respect for Harry. They have always given him stick, but when he was in the side, they couldn't say much. Now he is out of it, they feel their day has come and they don't need him. He had a terrible game in the five-a-side today. Stevie was on the same side, and moaning bitterly. 'How the hell can we win with that idiot in the team? How the hell could he have played 400 first-team games?' Gordon and I stirred it a bit, and encouraged him. But it is wrong. You worry about them when they can't see what a great professional Harry has been, and is.

5   Saturday Nights in Hell

27 October

Millwall 0   Middlesbrough 1

Today we got found out. The chickens came home to roost. We got a
hiding. After the euphoria of last Monday, the transformation was unbelievable.

Things started to go wrong in the first five minutes. Dennis knocked a
ball up for Hilly on the left wing. Hilly failed to read it and didn't go for
it. Dennis put his hands on his hips, his head bowed. 'What the hell . . .'
From then on he played half-heartedly. That left us to face the strongest
team in the league with ten players, four of them inexperienced youngsters.
It was a tight game, and in the early stages we needed all the help, all the
geeing up we could get. And there was no one to do it, Dennis having
abdicated.

After twenty minutes they were on top. We had a few flashes. Shots just
over the bar, dangerous-looking crosses easily cleared by Stuart Boam,
their centre half. They pushed the ball around in midfield, always threaten-
ing to thrust aside our defence. We were denied that crucial early goal
you expect at home. Weak sides usually concede an early goal which sets
you up, takes the pressure off for the afternoon. But this time the pressure
was staying on.

They weren't brilliant. Rather they were secure; mature, together pros.
Bobby Murdoch in midfield gives them an aura of calm, presenting an
illusion that they are impregnable. That is his great ability. To be composed on the ball. He isn't fast, he isn't strong in the tackle, he doesn't
hit a great long ball, he can't beat a man. But what he is great at, when
everyone else in this Division is going at ninety miles an hour, hitting
impossible balls, trying to squeeze things into spaces when it just is not on,

is being composed, and slowing it down. Knocking the fifteen- or twenty-yard ball, getting it back, and knocking it again. For half an hour I ran myself ragged jockeying Murdoch, who would push it to Souness or Foggon. They would knock it forward at the moment I lunged, committed to yet another fruitless tackle.

But we all had our problems to face. The young lads in particular. The full backs were uneasy on the ball, anxious on this their biggest occasion. They were feeling uneasy, isolated. On the wings Stevie and Hilly were getting nothing out of the full backs.

Dave Donaldson in particular was struggling. He is a good player. Skilful and confident, he could and should be one of the best backs in the Division. But he was getting caught in possession a lot. Nobody was showing to receive the ball from him, and being a good lad he was loath to take the coward's way out and punt long hopeful balls upfield. I decided to get as near to him as possible, showing for the ball, then knocking it back to him and playing him into the game. Which is what a midfield player should do in that situation.

We got into a two-on-two situation down near their corner flag. A situation for a quick one-two normally, but this time it wasn't quite on. I knocked the ball to Dave, checking back for the return instead of going forward because a defender had read it well. Dave knocked it forward, the defender picked it up, a quick break down field, and bang! In the back of our net. I felt sick. The lads looked at me, the crowd howled, Dennis put his hands on his hips.

The irony was that I had shouted to Dave to hold it. He knew that the blame was shared. But there it was, five minutes to half-time, o–1, and down to me. I felt utterly defeated.

At half-time no one said anything. Dave said he hadn't heard my call, and accepted that it was partly his fault. But the atmosphere was one of passive acceptance.

Middlesbrough were set up then. They contained us. They weren't ambitious, they weren't brilliant, but they were imposing. They were what I believed we could and should have been. What I thought we were going to be eight weeks ago. They have the great assets for success, in the Second Division particularly.

They were together. There was no doubt of that. They knew everyone was trying. They knew that they could make a mistake without the ball ending in the back of the net, without someone shouting 'Get in the bath.' That is what football is all about.

After an hour, I was pulled off. I didn't go into the dressing-room, I just sat and watched the rest of the game. I wasn't really upset. I was half in a daze, completely past caring. Gordon went on, and we never looked like scoring really.

Afterwards we got in the bath, and everyone was sick. Sick because we had had a hiding. It was only 1–0, but we had been outclassed. Which is very rare. Outclassed, out-thought and outfought. Even in the things we were good at, we struggled.

Even Gordon Hill was quiet. We all were. Dennis just shrugged. I was beyond being surprised or hurt by the game then. It was a blow I had half expected. It was finally obvious that we weren't going to achieve anything really. It was a moment of awakening, of realization. This was what the good sides were like, and any pretensions we might have had at the beginning of the season, with the side we had then playing well, were gone.

Benny didn't say a word after the game. Normally he would have a go at us. But he just stood there. He was sick. But he wasn't alive enough to have a go. It was a general feeling of being deadened.

You get beaten a lot of times in football. But a few times it is conclusive. Comprehensive. We were stuffed. It is not the game people think. You might get beaten 3–0 and you think 'Christ, we competed well. They got the crucial breaks and we were a little bit unlucky.' And people laugh at you. But you know that you have struck at their heart a few times and the goalkeeper has maybe saved them, or you have missed a couple of chances. But I can't say we had a chance in the whole game against Middlesbrough.

Dennis having been up at Hull, you now knew he was going to go, whatever the terms. Getting them sorted out was the reason for the delay in his signing. Now he would definitely go. If there was any one of us offered a contract by another club, we would sign today, whatever the terms. The Den was a place to get out of today. I didn't even go into the tea-room afterwards. I just went home.

Sandra is always waiting at the door, looking to see my face. And I said 'I've been pulled off again.' And she said 'Oh no. What happened?' And I could not tell her. Telling would just have been repeating the afternoon's hurt, so I said 'Don't worry, love. I'm getting away.'

I can't face putting myself into a position where I can be hurt like that again. It isn't only me. All the lads must have felt the same. But I was the one pulled off, which makes it worse really. I've been so intensely involved down there for so long, and now it is clear that the end of our side is near. Dennis is obviously going to go, Gordon is half out of the side, Harry and Bryan Brown are out, we've got some new young lads in. It was going to be a make-or-break season for us, and now it is obviously break.

With each passing week, I'm deteriorating back into that dreadful limbo where your confidence goes, your belief in yourself is eroded, your appetite for the game diminishes. Deep down inside I believe that I can play. I know I could succeed, achieve something in my career. But I am convinced that what happens to a player is conditioned almost totally by what happens around him in his club. Good management, good leadership means a good morale and a good team.

And at the moment, at Millwall, we have little that is good in terms of influence. There is a lot of character, a lot of skill in the team, but it has no chance of coming out because of our bad organization.

29 October

A failed football club in October. A depressing place. Already, with seven months to go, the morning becomes a dread. There was a terrible, flat atmosphere this morning. Everybody felt numbed by Saturday's game, the rosy optimism of last week totally gone.

Normally we would have a crisis meeting. A 'Where do we go from here' meeting. But we didn't. We trained normally. Benny had nothing to say.

30 October

When the teamsheet went up for tomorrow's game, Gordon was out, Dennis was out and I was twelfth man. Mickey Kelly and Dougy Allder are in. Franky Saul is still in the wilderness. Kingy is doubtful but we've got Steve Sherwood on loan from Chelsea, so Derek Smethurst is saved from playing in goal!

Dennis has gone to Hull, which is no surprise after Saturday. From the team it is obvious that Benny has made his mind up that all of us from the old team are out. All the trouble-makers, as he would call us – Dennis, me, Gordon, Harry, Franky, Brownie. Alfie, Kitch and Alan are the most experienced players in the side. They and Kingy are about all that is left.

It is probably the least painful dropping of my life. There is nothing I can identify with any more. It is a new era, a new bunch of kids. And there is nothing there for me. The only question is how to get away. Gordon feels the same. Although we were theoretically competing for the same place in the side, he was not too unhappy at being out.

I suspect that Benny has had these changes in his mind for a long time. When after two good wins the club captain goes to Hull to talk terms, there is obviously a transition going on in Benny's head. The team is obviously broken up, and he is going to give the young lads a chance. I think he had these changes in his mind all along. Where at the start of the season I was hoping that we would become a good promotion-challenging side, he would see it in terms of breaking it up. He hadn't rushed to bring either Dougy or Dennis back when they were out of the side. I think he was thinking of these youngsters – Ned Kelly, Gordon Hill, Stevie Brown, David Donaldson and Eddie Jones – as the basis of a new side. And really, instead of looking for an excuse to keep the old side together, he was looking for an excuse to break it up. So the results have helped him. The Middlesbrough result justifies him in dropping me and selling Dennis.

I think it is premature. I think it is completely wrong to let a good side, a nice blend, a lot of experience and some good young players, go to waste. I think Benny is wrong. I think his new team will struggle. I don't think some of the lads he has brought into the side have got the character. A couple of them are clowns, who really should be educated about the game before they take the place of good experienced professionals like the Gordons and the Harrys of this world. Especially as they can have learnt very little on the way through because there has been no real coaching. They have learnt nothing.

So they are going to have to learn as they go along, which I don't think is a very good way. It is a good way for one or even two young players to learn. But if there are four or five in the side at the same time it doesn't work.

When Dougy came into our side, that was fine, because he had a lot of experienced players around him, and he could absorb things playing with us. And we could carry him a little while he learnt. But now Dougy is the teacher. And he is not really experienced enough to be that. There's Alfie. But he is an individualist in his style, so he won't be able to help much. You can't, with five or six at once. Alan and Kitch will have to grow into teachers, and they will very quickly. But it is too much, too quickly. It is not transition, it is revolution.

1 November

Millwall 1   Bolton Wanderers 1

Two weeks after the previous League Cup game at Forest, and how things have changed. After the euphoria of that moment, a real downer. I was sub last night. Before the game the sub goes through all sorts of emotions. One minute you think 'Perhaps I'll go on and score the winning goal.' The next you worry that you'll sit there freezing to death while the lads win 5–0.

Neither happened. I sat on the bench with Lawrie and Jack Blackman. Lawrie isn't too bad. He doesn't shout and scream like some trainers. Jack has got a favourite saying: 'Push up, lads.' I sat between them keeping my own counsel. It was a lousy game. Lots of endeavour and mis-placed passes. It would be easy to pick holes in people's performances, but I know what it's like out there, and so I refrained from dishing out stick, apart from the odd raised eyebrow. Just before half-time we got a penalty, which Dougy missed. Only justice, because it was a terrible decision. Bolton's manager, Jimmy Armfield, was going spare. 'Would you believe this referee,' he kept yelling. And we sympathized. Then Clarky scored, and that looked enough for me. The first one usually is at the Den. It looked like I wouldn't be needed.

Bolton equalized early in the second half. We were surprised. And then they started to play a bit. There is a phone in the dug-out linked to Benny's seat in the directors' box. And it starts. 'Ring ring.' 'Yes, boss, yes, boss.' The orders pour into Lawrie's ear. 'OK, boss. Right.'

'Ned, Ned, NED,' Lawrie screams, 'get a grip. Get hold of it.'

We've lost control in midfield, and Ned doesn't look as if he can rectify matters.

'Ring, ring.' It's Benny again. Perhaps he wants me on.

'Yes, boss, right, boss, OK.'

'Give it to Hilly.' Benny's orders are relayed to the nearest player, who pretends not to hear.

'Push up,' yells Jack.

'Shut up,' thinks I.

'Ring, ring.' Bolton are looking as if they might nick it now. Is this the call? It must be. No! The second half went on like this. We were so bad in the second half, with Bolton pushing it around in complete ease in midfield, I was convinced every time the phone rang that I was on. But no. The phone went continuously, moves were ordered and counter-ordered, with none of them getting through to the lads on the field.

With ten minutes to go, it was clear that in spite of the mediocre performance, my services weren't going to be required, so I made my way to the dressing-room. The crowd were very discontented by this time, and made their point by giving me a cheer. But that is meaningless. It was just a way of protesting.

After the game everyone was muttering. Bill Nelan, one of the directors, came up to me in the tea-room. 'What is going on?' he asked. 'I just don't know what he is playing at.' Which is fairly standard. What was more worrying was that Gordon Borland, the secretary, said exactly the same thing. And he is a good politician. If he is turning against Benny, maybe Benny's days are numbered. Certainly with the team he has got at the moment, he could be facing a struggle against relegation. And that could leave him jobless. I wouldn't be surprised to see him out within two months.

And that would sadden me. Because although I don't want to be part of it any more, Benny is someone I can sympathize with. I think he is wrong. But I would hate to see him become the victim of backstage whispering and boardroom intrigue.

2 November

I haven't spoken to Benny all week. I can't summon up the emotion for a confrontation. It seems so bloody childish to go into the office and start asking for explanations. In spite of my reputation as a trouble-maker, that is something I've never done. I've gone in there all right, but not to ask 'Why am I dropped, boss?' Team selection is his job.

So I'm still on the sheet today, as twelfth man. Harry is coming with us up to Notts County as thirteenth man.

Franky Saul is really fed up. He is great in practice games, but even now that Denny has gone and I'm dropped he is still not getting in the side. He can't understand what he has to do, to get a game. Bill Nelan passed the rumour back through the grapevine that he was the chairman's signing, not Benny's, and Benny never wanted him at the club. He was signed as our insurance when we were going for promotion two years ago. The story is that Benny wanted someone else, but they couldn't raise the money, so Purser went out and bought Franky off his own bat. And Benny has never rated him. It's amazing the way that sort of thing happens in football clubs. The incredible thing is the way Franky is developing. Normally, by the time you reach our age, you can't really develop. But he is adding real vision to his game. He is a fine player, and really ought to be in the side. If any of the lads were to pick a side, he would be in it.

After training today Franky went into the office to see Benny. We were all getting our clothes on, and he said 'I'm going to see him.' He was not only out of the side but Benny had not even put him on the sheet so that he could get £25 for himself. Benny has really bummed him out.

You always wait on a Friday morning for the teamsheet to go up. If you have won the previous week you know Benny won't change the side, but the lads out of the team are always hoping to be twelfth or thirteenth man, which means they get the appearance money and the bonus. And it means you are back in it a little bit. When you are in the side you always think that you wouldn't want to be twelfth man. I don't want it. But when you are out of it for a month you are delighted to be twelfth man. At least 'he' has noticed you. And you get the money too.

So Franky was sweating there, saying 'If I'm not on the sheet I'm going to see him today. I'll chin him. I will.' He is a bit hot-tempered. The sheet came down and Harry and I were on it, which of course made it worse. Because Franky knew my feelings about not wanting to be involved, and whenever Harry is on the sheet everyone else moans. So Franky went storming upstairs.

We were having a cup of tea in the little room outside Benny's office. And we heard the door go crash as he went in. Ten minutes later crash again and he came out.

We expected to see Benny on a stretcher. But it is a terrible thing seeing Benny. He is a bit like Busby. The great thing about Busby was that you would go in there fighting and full of demands. And he would give you nothing at all. He might even take a tenner off your wages. And you would come out thinking 'What a great guy.' I remember going in there once absolutely livid. And ten minutes later I came out, no better off, walking on air. Delighted.

Benny is a bit like that. He doesn't quite have the charisma Busby had. You don't come out walking on air. But he neutralizes everything you say. You go in with a clear-cut list of grievances. Unanswerable complaints which you had worked out before going in. You think 'He'll have to concede this is true.' Because it is. And you would go in there and lay it all down. And he would talk his way out of it. And you come out, not feeling happy, but thwarted. He has done you. But he has not done you in a way which enabled you to get it off your chest. He has conned you. No matter how determined you are, he cons you. Fobs you off with some promise or other. Or you make your point, and he says 'Ah, yes. But . . .' He will never have a go back. If he did, you could have a row, which would be much better. You would get it off your chest. But with him you always come out, and, like someone after a Chinese meal, twenty minutes later you are hungry again. You want to go back in. I'd get in my car and be half-way home, and suddenly think 'He's conned me. I'm going back.' But if you did, you would get the same treatment.

Which Franky obviously had. He came out and had a cup of tea. And he was still saying 'One day, I'll hit him.'

3 November

Notts County 3   Millwall 3

Going as twelfth or thirteenth man is a drag. The thirteenth man is the one who normally gets the worst of it. You are in effect skip-boy, helping Jack Blackman with the kit on and off the coach, laying the shirts out before the game, making sure the lads have chewing gum, tie-ups, tea at half-time. A load of menial little tasks, a lesson in unobtrusive suffering.

That should have been Harry's job. He is a funny lad. He hides his feelings under that big smile, but as I was helping him with the clothes, our eyes met and I knew he was sharing my 'What are we doing here?' thoughts.

About 2.15 everything was laid out, nothing for me to do. At this stage the lads are getting geed up, slowly departing into a world of their own. Benny as always was moving around giving instructions. Time for the non-combatants to get out of the way. I went out for a quiet tea underneath the stand. A chance to have a cup of tea, a Kit-Kat, and to contemplate which suicide method to use.

Two of the young girls who follow us around were in there. They are nice kids who go to any lengths to see the lads play. Their loyalty never ceases to amaze me. They travel on those old coaches, setting out from London at ridiculous hours sometimes. If we are playing at Carlisle or Middlesbrough they have to travel through the night and still do so. They have time off from work, spend their pocket money on travel instead of new dresses, and in general build their lives around the Millwall fixture list. We know them. At least we know their faces, taking their support for granted most of the time. Sometimes rushing from a train or coach we spare them a moment to talk and laugh. A casual word from us, a moment to savour for them.

They came straight up to me. 'Hello, Eamon. What's the matter, love, not playing?' They were slightly embarrassed, probably seeing the hurt. 'How's the baby?' They know I've become a dad, just as they know all the little bits and pieces about the lads. One of them had given me a present when Timothy was born. It was a little cardigan. I was really moved.

'Is Gordon playing?'

It leapt out of her mouth. Gordon Hill is their new pin-up.

'Yes, love, he's playing.'

'Isn't he gorgeous. What is he like?'

I wanted to say 'Dumb like the rest of us at eighteen' but didn't. Instead the inevitable chit-chat. 'He's a nice lad, not as good-looking as me, though'; 'No, I don't think he has a girl friend' – a reply which they want to hear. By then it was time for me to go and change, so I left, with them saying 'Hope you are back in the team soon.' Which they really mean. If they had their way, we would all play. Still they had cheered me up.

I sat on the bench next to Harry. At least I wouldn't have to suffer alone. Ned Kelly was playing in midfield with Dougy Allder, and with the two new full backs, and with Stevie Brown and Gordon Hill in the side, it looked like the reserve side we faced in pre-season practice games. Steve Sherwood was in goal for his second game, as Kingy is still injured.

Notts County looked really impressive for the first fifteen minutes. Big, strong and sharp, they looked a useful side. Harry and I exchanged glances. It might turn out to be a good day after all.

Notts went one up after twenty minutes. A bad mistake by Steve Sherwood. They deserved it. Masson was pulling all the strings in midfield, and for the rest of the half it was all one-way traffic. We were playing terribly. Harry and I were having a whale of a time; sly nudges and grins. It was so one-sided it wasn't true. But half-time came with the score 1–0. On the ropes, but not yet quite knocked out.

Benny greeted the lads in the dressing-room. 'Well done, my sons. You're OK. Just keep going, keep playing football.' Gordon Hill was sitting there, his head in his hands. Fannying. 'What's the matter, son?' 'I dunno, boss. I just can't seem to get it right.' 'Don't worry, son. It'll come. Keep it going.' I had a quiet grin on my face. It didn't look as if it would come right by Christmas, if they kept playing till then. Benny saw me, as he was talking to Gordon, and looked across sharply. 'What's the matter with you?' 'Me? Nothing, boss.'

The second half starts with a similar pattern, and soon County went 2–0 up. The knock-out. But we start pushing it around a bit. I couldn't see us scoring though, until one of their defenders gives away this unbelievable penalty. So Dougy scored. 2–1. But still, although we were playing a bit, I didn't think we would do it. It still looked like a home win. Then Ned Kelly, who had been doing well, picked up the ball in midfield, advanced unchallenged and let one go from thirty yards. The net bulged. It was an unbelievable goal.

After that we started getting on top. Harry and I started feeling sick. But Benny is anxious now, pulling people back, feeling well pleased with a draw, as well he might be. With ten minutes to go, County took the lead again, this time against the run of play. 'Phew', the relief. By losing possession Gordon Hill had given County the chance to win the game, confirming all our prejudices against him. Two minutes to go, and we made our last desperate lunge at the County goal. Just as I was thinking 'No way', Stevie crossed, the ball bobbled around the box, and Gordon Hill stuck it in the net. 3–3.

The game was over, and the dressing-room was filled with jubilation.

'Get us a beer, Eamon,' young Ned shouted. I smiled a sickly smile and did so. Benny was ecstatic, flying high while the lads were in the bath. I helped Jack Blackman collect the kit, all the sweaty jock-straps, muddy boots, dirty shirts. Then as the lads emerged scrubbed and glowing with happiness, and Harry and I stood forlorn in the corner, Benny started.

'Out in the park. That's what this game is all about.' He was strolling around, addressing nobody in particular. 'It's all right shooting your mouth off about tactics, or politics, but it is out there you've got to do it. Talking won't help you out there.' The bullets were aimed at me, but I wasn't biting. I was smiling at Harry, who, sensing the possibility of a confrontation, looked as if he was wishing he had gone for a drink.

'What's the matter, son, what are you so pleased about?'

'I'm pleased for you, boss,' said I, half mockingly.

'Good, good. Are you really?' He didn't sound sure.

'Yes, of course. The lads did well. Bit of luck and we could have won it.'

In spite of my treacherous thoughts during the game, I really did mean it. I am pleased for him in a way. I still like Benny in spite of all that has happened over the years. Watching him then surrounded by his new, young, obedient team, and with a good result behind him, you feel for him. He was triumphant. Normally an emotional man, but very unsure of much of what he did, he was so delighted when things went right. A fifty-year-old kid with a new toy which he had suddenly discovered the workings of.

Then he went to the boardroom in triumph to knock down a couple of celebratory Scotches and tell them how he had done it.

In the dressing-room Ned was telling us how he had done it from thirty yards. 'Like it, Eamon? That's the way to hit 'em, eh? Bang, get in!' He was over the moon. He had every right to be. I looked around. No Dennis, no Gordon Bolland, no Bryan Brown, no Harry, and today no Kingy. Who would have believed it a month ago?

On the coach back, another sign of the times. Harry and I were the only remaining members of the card-school. All the young lads were still high on success, discussing loudly where to celebrate when we got back to town. Harry and I were left with our thoughts, interrupted only by Benny still high on the victory. 'What was great today was nobody packed it in.

Everyone kept going when we were under the collar. We'll do better now that Burnett has gone.'

Benny hasn't changed. How many times have we heard that farewell?

5 November

Signs of the times at training today. Lawrie set up this routine where we were divided into groups of three. Each with a ball. You interpass it down the field from the half-way line, and then one goes wide to knock it into the box for the other two to score. It is a ridiculous routine anyway. I was in the group with Kitch. What is the point of Kitch going wide and knocking it to me in the six-yard box? He is never going to get into that position on a Saturday. It is a function for the sake of doing a function, as opposed to one to eliminate a basic fault in your team.

But another group had Harry, Ned and Stevie in it. Harry, however worthless the exercise, will always do it. The reason he has lasted so long is that he feels that there is a value in it. And Stevie and Ned were mucking around. So he got really angry and started rucking them. They despise his values, and he is the only person at Millwall who ever tries to encourage people. But they said 'Piss off, Harry. Who needs you.' Ned said 'You need this, because you are limited. We don't need it.' And it got really abusive. In the end Stevie said 'You're just a foreman'. They have always been fairly scornful of Harry. But it is sad to see a great pro being scoffed at by these lads.

I had tea with Harry, Gordon and Franky afterwards. Harry was still upset about the row. The one comfort we all feel is that we are all out of favour together. In a way we support one another.

It is funny how quickly the hierarchy in the dressing-room can change. Now that Dennis is gone, and we're all out of the side, Alfie is becoming king.

6 November

The first team went up to Bolton today for the League Cup replay tonight. The only change from Saturday was Gordon getting on the sheet instead of me as twelfth man.

7 November

Orient Reserves 2   Millwall Reserves 4

Back in the bloody Midweek League again. It's an unbelievable sensation going to play at Orient on a Wednesday afternoon in November. There is no one there, absolutely nothing at stake, except your own pride. You don't feel like it at all. And whereas for two hours before a first-team game you are beginning to get nervous, beginning to get geed up, feeling a bit of tension and atmosphere, here you go to a ground which is empty. It is like a graveyard. You have to walk around a bit to find where to go in – especially at Orient.

When you do get in there, the dressing-rooms are cold, because they don't bother switching on the heating for the Midweek League. They get no gate, of course, so they do it as cheaply as they can.

I never start getting changed until half an hour beforehand anyway, but even then you feel absolutely empty. No tension at all. Not a glimmer of excitement. Today we had a decent side – Gordon, Harry, Bryan Brown, Franky, all in the reserves. All in the doghouse. All a bit sick. Made worse by the fact that the first team won yesterday. Gordon went up as sub yesterday, but he didn't get on, so he came to play for us. He gave us all the bad news, told us how they had done.

So we don't fancy it at all. And you know it is going to be hard because they have a young side who are going to run themselves into the ground, particularly when they see some first-team names in our side. That will make them have even more of a go.

We were all in the dressing-room trying to build up some sort of feeling. Which is where Harry is so good. He would be the same on Hackney Marshes. He was still geed up, walking around saying 'Come on, we've got to have a go. There's £2 at stake.'

You have got to think of a million different ways to motivate yourself. Really it is down to personal pride. And possibly that there might be a scout in the stand just having a look. And you might impress him. But it is all very intangible. It is very hard to get hold of something and say 'Right, let's have a go.'

But if you don't, you are struggling. Because you go out, and there is no crowd, and the pitch is bumpy. Particularly at Orient. What a terrible place! It was cold. A Wednesday afternoon in November, you should be watching *Crossroads* or something, preferably the racing. But you should be somewhere warm. Not there.

And if you go out there not too bothered about the whole thing, thinking you will play it off the cuff, all of a sudden you find you are 2–0 down. Which we did. And you feel as sick as a pig. You think now you really have got to work, because there is an hour to go, and unless you absolutely stop altogether, you are going to get a horrible chasing. So why not go out and have a go?

And you begin to enjoy it. It is amazing the pleasure you can get out of it. Even more than the first team. Because once you start to get involved, there is no stomach-wrenching pressure. It's just your own pride, and you begin to enjoy the game.

Franky and I were in midfield. Franky always has a go. He never jacks it in. He will always want to have a go, to get involved. So we had a go.

Gordon was impossible. He had been up to Bolton yesterday, and was probably a bit tired anyway. He saw the 'new coming' which probably made him even more sick. So he wouldn't run, he wouldn't get involved at all. I had a real go at him at one stage. He just shrugged his shoulders. I couldn't say any more, because I knew how he felt. No way could I get self-righteous about it.

So we went two down, even though some of us were having a go. Harry was having a go, but there was this little right winger who was giving him the biggest chasing of his life. Harry was kicking him all over the park. They were a good side with a lot of good young players.

At half-time we went into the dressing-room and Benny was there. We hadn't seen him before the game. He didn't say anything. He just stood in the corner. They won last night, so really he doesn't give a damn how we do today. In fact he looked smug, as if he was pleased we were struggling. As if he was thinking 'My young lads did it last night. Look at you lot!'

Billy Neill was in charge. And it was difficult for him to have a go at us, because we are his contemporaries. He is used to having a young side. He can have a go at them. But he knows how Gordon feels. And Benny was casting his shadow over things. Because he wouldn't say anything himself, but his presence stopped anyone else from saying anything.

So we went out again. And we were still getting a chasing, but after fifteen minutes we pulled one back. Then we got a penalty. Then Gordon got this brilliant goal. He still wasn't bothering, but perhaps all the rucking he was taking was getting through to him, and he started doing a little bit more. And he picked up this ball about thirty-five yards out, took it past two men and hit it from twenty-five yards into the top corner. A brilliant goal. I was delighted. He is such a good player, and it is sickening to see a class player, who could have played at the very highest level, struggling.

Then we nicked another one before the end, so we won 4–2.

We came off the park really pleased. It is meaningless. The Midweek League. They hardly even bother to print the result in the paper. But you come off with a little glow of satisfaction. Because you have got a little bit of self-respect back.

Benny came in afterwards. 'Well done, that was better. See you to-morrow.' And he was off. You haven't really shown him, but you feel as if you have.

Which is all very petty. But that is what being in the reserves means. You are looking all the time for chances to thumb your nose at people. It is a petty little league, and if you are in it for long you become a petty little person. It is the horror for players in and around London. Playing in that league is death.

Robin Wainwright was playing today. I think he could be a good player, but he has only had a couple of first-team games. He is a good lad, he has kept going, even though he had to wait nine months for his chance, and then came straight back out again after two games. He has played in the reserves for all this time. I couldn't. I'd pack up the game rather than that. I'd have to. It is too soul-destroying.

8 November

Yesterday Benny was quoted as saying that his new young side is going to be Millwall's best. The best side he has had since he has been there. With Dennis gone, and Harry, Gordon, Bryan Brown, Franky Saul and myself in the reserves it is certainly a new side. And when I look at the potential we had at the beginning of this season, the delicate balance which has been destroyed, I feel sick.

But I also feel part of it no more. I'm leaving. I went to see Benny today, and asked for a transfer. He started off by trying to soothe me, saying I was too good a player for him to let go, that I still had a part to play (a bit part?), and all the normal flannel. I was reluctant to do it, but in the end I told him he had a team of clowns, and that he was a con-man, and I wanted no more part of it. And I don't. I shall get back in the team if I stay here. But I want to go somewhere where I can be involved. I either want to be wholly in something or right out of it. And there is no way I can be involved here any more.

When I told Benny he was a con-man, he said 'Do you really mean that?'

'Yes.'

'Right, son. That's you and me finished. We had a relationship. But that is you and me finished. From now on you are no different to any other player.'

A shame. I like Benny. And I fear for him. If he survives the season with this team, I'll be surprised. But I don't want to stay around and watch. Our dream, the Millwall dream, is over for me.

9 November

As we don't have a match tomorrow, we got extra training when the first team had finished. We have to do weights. I don't believe in weight-training anyway. But it means that by the time you get in, the bath is cold and full of slime, someone has used your towel, and everyone has left already, and it really gets to you. You think 'What am I doing here?' All you have got to look forward to is Aldershot reserves away next Wednesday.

You are getting the thin end of the wedge all over the place. Your wages are about £40 lighter a week. So you really begin to wonder at the point of it all. Especially if you have been used to the first team so that your best mate has left an hour before you. You feel bitter and out of it.

The person who is really suffering is Brownie. He seems distressed to the point where he can't react at all. He hasn't been able to gee himself up to perform in the reserves. His reaction seems to be to flick the ball up and whack it over the stands rather than buckle down and say 'I'll show them.' He has got even more overweight, more irresponsible. And that is sad, because he has the ability to be an outstanding full back by Second Division standards. A good First Division player even. Yet he is a Midweek League player now, and looks to have settled for that.

10 November

Millwall 2   Cardiff City 0

I didn't go to watch. I stayed at home. I'm only at Millwall in body now, not in spirit. I'm not interested in how the first team got on, apart from some snide desire to see them stuffed. I couldn't go and sit in the stand hoping for them to get beaten. It is too small-minded for words. So I watched the racing on telly instead.

What is terrible is that it is only November. There were ninety-two League clubs taking the field today, and I wasn't part of it. I was sitting at home watching the lousy racing.

On a Saturday the lack of involvement is terrible. At 12 o'clock I had breakfast, bacon, egg, sausage, toast and tea. And it felt wrong. I should have been having scrambled eggs. A little thing like that makes you very conscious you aren't in it.

At 1 o'clock you think 'I should be going to the ground now'. Saturday afternoon drags. It is a weird feeling not playing on a Saturday afternoon. After ten years as a first-team player, doing the same things, going through the same rituals, your whole body and mind are geared to doing this every week.

On Fridays you have steak for dinner because it is good for you. And you go to bed early because it is good for you. You stay chaste because it is good for you. Your whole life has a point.

And that point is 3 o'clock on a Saturday afternoon. Your life is very purposeful. And when you aren't playing, there is a big void.

13 November

It is strange how relationships change, ever so slightly. With Dennis gone, and the rest of us older players out of the side, Alf is king in the dressing-room. Kitch is the new captain, but he is a quiet lad, and never has that much to say. So Alfie is the one who complains, says we should do this and we shouldn't do that. A role that Dennis and I used to fill.

Everyone has their little weakness that the other players latch on to, to give them stick about. The joke about Alfie is that he is very careful with money. It is a stock joke, which he plays along with, that you never catch him at the bar. When we were down in Torquay, we had one classic Alfie story. He and Dougy came in earlier than the rest of us one night, and Alfie ordered a pot of tea. As it arrived, four or five of us came in too. We joined him at the table and said 'Oh, we'll have a cup of that.' And Alfie said 'It'll cost you 6p a cup.' And he meant it. He collected the money.

One of the lads told me today that after the game on Saturday the news had come through that Hull had lost. It was Dennis's first game for them and their first defeat for several weeks. Benny's reaction had been predictably ecstatic.

14 November

Millwall Reserves 4 Peterborough Reserves 1

I geed myself up by thinking: 'Maybe Noel Cantwell is here. I'd like to play for Peterborough. I don't care what division they are in. And even if I don't go there I would like to think that he is sitting in the stand wondering "What is a good player like that doing in the Midweek League?" '

I played great. I was doing things on the ball – magic. And I scored direct from a free kick. Curled it round the wall into the top corner from just outside the box. Which gave me enormous pleasure, as it did the three OAPS who were sitting in the stand.

I enjoyed the game aesthetically in a way that you never can a League game. I enjoyed doing a little on the ball, flicking it over people's heads and half-volleying it out to the wing, that sort of thing. Back to childhood again – just playing for personal enjoyment, for the sheer joy of doing something well. That is missing from League football. There your motives are much more base. The battle for points, league position and bonus is something which doesn't exist in the reserves.

But I could never settle for reserve-team football. I left Manchester United, when they were the greatest club in the country, to go to York so I could get first-team football. I'd go down to a Third Division team now for first-team football. The thing that has always kept me out of the

Midweek League and kept me in first teams is my insatiable desire to be in them. Not ability. I've got no more ability than most people, it is just desire, desire, desire.

15 November

I was watching one of the apprentices this morning. He is a young boy who has been at the club a couple of years as an apprentice, and has just signed as a professional. But he has got absolutely no chance of making it. He really is the butt of everything. You get such lads in every club, who haven't got a lot of ability possibly. They have a fair amount, enough to get taken on in the first place, but not enough to look like they are ever going to make it. And they have no way of compensating for that by being one of the lads or being particularly good at anything.

They get it during the week in the five-a-sides. Everyone gets at them. You get a lad who is last pick every morning. You pick up sides. And it ends up with the same two lads standing there for the last two places. And it is the same every morning of their lives. There is a moment of complete rejection every day, their fellow professionals saying 'I don't want you in my side.' That is a comment on their whole career. And when the game starts, if things start going wrong, everyone blames them. Everyone slags them off.

This particular boy is dead honest, a nice lad. He works really hard at the game. He never shirks anything, he gets involved as best he can. But it all comes to the same in the end. He has got absolutely no chance of making it. He is a certainty to get a free transfer at the end of the season. And there are lots of lads like that. They come in at fifteen from school, and you get maybe one out of every ten who is going to make a League player. And for the rest the next three years is going to be one long agony. A long-drawn-out process of not making it at a crucial time in their lives. A time when your confidence can either grow so that you can grow into being a man, or when you can be really destroyed if the wrong things happen to you.

And football clubs are notoriously insensitive to people's feelings. Because it is a whole group thing, and at times pretty brutal. Being a footballer means that some marvellous things happen to you. But for those who don't do so well, agonizing things can happen too. And there is nobody around in a football club to say 'Never mind, son', or to try and understand how they feel.

The way the game treats young players is a disgrace. It is one of the really shameful aspects of the game. Not only that they are not doing well as players, but that they aren't getting any preparation for the inevitable end when they are eighteen or nineteen or twenty. When they are kicked out or given a free transfer. They aren't given any education, they aren't prepared for any trade. They are on the streets. And worst of all really, the kind of lifestyle they have is completely undisciplined. The day finishes at lunch-time, so they arse around for the rest of the day in betting shops, or watching TV or whatever. The whole thing, far from being a preparation for going out into life, is a complete negation of everything you will have to be when you have got to go to a nine-to-five job. The shock they experience must be frightful. And coming on top of all the abuse they have had to suffer and all the shattered dreams they have had, it is a very crushing process.

Sometimes you see the dad and family and friends at reserve-team matches. And the kid might not know what is going on, but the families must know. There is no progress to report. Their greatest day is the day they sign on. Every day after that it is getting worse and worse.

I remember seeing a kid break down and cry. He was seventeen. Because the moment of truth for them is on their seventeenth or eighteenth birthday, when they have to be signed or released. This is the moment they have built up to ever since they signed as an apprentice. The moment they have worked for. At a club like Millwall they don't get any preparation. They get no coaching, very little assistance. The whole thing at Millwall throughout the years I've been there has been geared to one thing only – the first team. And the thing is, not only will the lads suffer in a personal sense, and feel the bitter rejection, but the club will suffer. There is nothing surer than that the club will decline because of a lack of young players coming through. That may seem a silly thing to say when people like Stevie Brown and Mickey Kelly are in the first team. But those youngsters illustrate it too. They have got plenty of talent, but they have been developed in the wrong environment. They haven't had the leadership, the coaching, or the right environment to grow in. So I don't believe they will make it. They haven't been developed as players, and they haven't been exposed to the right values. So everyone suffers from this policy of expediency, of looking after the immediate thing, the first team.

And it is so wasteful. Because all the time there is this fantastic raw material. No matter what anybody says, once kids are good enough to be signed on, a lot of them are good enough to make it. The difference between making it and not making it is the amount of time spent with them, the amount of effort put into helping them to become players. And the amount of opportunity they are given. So it is not as if you are discarding people who wouldn't be any use to you. Because they could save you hundreds of thousands of pounds in the end.

This kid I saw crying had just been up in the office with Benny, and Benny had had to tell him that he was being released. Benny did not like doing it, I know. He is quite a kind-hearted man in his way. But the kid was sitting out on the wall by the touchline, crying. I just happened to go out and saw him. I tried to tell him this was not the end of the road, and he could still have a decent life, that football is only a game, and so on. But it meant nothing to him at the time. In the end I got him fixed up with a catering class at the college. I think he was going to try and become a chef. I don't know whether it worked out or not. You don't. They just go, and that is the last you see of them.

It is desolation for them. And it is a commentary on some of the attitudes in football. You rarely get through to people in football if you start talking about this kind of thing. People say 'Yes, but they know what they are doing when they come into it.' But do they? At fifteen, I didn't know what I was doing when I went into it. You come from a working-class home with no future except as factory fodder. No real education and no real choices available to you. So if someone comes along and says 'Would you like to be a footballer?', of course you would. But is that a choice? It is something that you fall into.

And who is responsible? The parents obviously have a certain responsibility. But I think the game does too. Because if you want to be a big deal, which we do, which we claim, then along with being a big deal goes having big responsibilities. And we do not meet them for young people at all.

A lot of the flash guys going around now, who have made it in the First Division and who shame the game with their behaviour, are that way because they came out of this kind of mess. And if we are ever going to have a decent game, present a decent image, we are going to have to start working with the young people in the game. Giving them a sense of responsibility to the club and to the game. And that can only come when you have a sense of responsibility towards them.

I was at a function last night. Tommy Sampson was there. And all the first team. We were all in a group. And this guy came up, a supporter. He was a bit drunk. And he said to Tommy 'You are Brian Clark, aren't you?' 'No,' said Tommy. 'My name is Tommy Sampson.' 'Oh, yes,' said the supporter. 'You've never really made it, have you?' Tommy hasn't, yet. He is a good lad. He still has a chance. He has been a bit unlucky. Luckier than some, unluckier than most. But this supporter just crushed him. Dreadful. We all laughed at the time. Tommy laughed too. But it was a terrible thing.

16 November

Gordon Bolland is back in the side, and Franky is substitute, as Stevie Brown is injured.

Your week is really awkward when you are a reserve. You play on Wednesday. So you can't do much training on Tuesday. You play on Wednesday when the first team have the day off. And you are off on Thursday when they are back in. And you come back and work hard on a Friday when they are having an easy day in preparation for Saturday. You completely lose touch with everything.

Physically you are cut off. You are supposed to go to the games on a Saturday, but no one really cares whether you are there or not. There is no suggestion of kidding you that you are part of it by taking a squad of players to all the games. You are out of it, and no one cares whether you go to the games or not. 'The No. 10 is dead, long live the No. 10.' Which is part of the game. But you are going to need the people you drop some time. You are going to need them through injury or whatever some time. So every time you screw them when they are out of it, you are screwing yourself.

You have got to keep them in all the tactical talks, all the training sessions, because otherwise you are going to lose them. And when you lose people, you can't get them back again.

It's just a matter of organization and consideration. But you ought to show consideration for all your staff anyway. Gordon and Harry have done great for the club. They deserve consideration. It is different if it is a lad who has done nothing. But for people who have played over 200 games for you, it shouldn't be like throwing them out of a lifeboat. Because you are going to need them at some stage. Gordon is back in tomorrow, for example.

But Benny has obviously decided it is time for change. He hardly bothers to speak to Gordon or Franky now. And he must have decided he has no more use for them, because it is unusual for him to do that.

But it is the aimless Saturdays which are the worst thing. At Manchester it was not so bad, because the reserve team played in the Central League, which meant that you had your Saturday filled. And it gave you a similar cycle to a first-team player. You didn't feel so cut off. And the Central League, or down here the Football Combination, is better football too. The Midweek League is death on every level.

17 November

Crystal Palace 1   Millwall 1

I spent the afternoon at London Broadcasting as a studio guest. It provided some purpose, but I hated it. I felt as if I were betraying myself. Walking through the City to LBC was horrible. The City is terrible on a Saturday afternoon. It is like death, no one around. I was thinking 'Jesus, what am I doing here? They are playing at Palace. A local derby with a big crowd, and a great atmosphere. And I'm going to *talk* about the game.' Those dismal streets reflected my mood exactly.

And of course when I got there I was hoping to be told that Palace were stuffing Millwall. But I went through the door, and Ian Marshall, the Sports Editor, came rushing up with a slip in his hand. 'Here is good news for you, Eamon. Millwall are 1–0 up.' So I said 'Great.'

Sitting in the studio waiting to go on, I could hear the match report coming through. It sounded a great game. End to end, exciting stuff. And there was I sitting in a poxy studio. I felt terrible. But Palace got an equalizer, which made me feel better.

20 November

Charlton Reserves 2   Millwall Reserves 3

Playing in Midweek League football is futile enough at the best of times. But playing Midweek League football at the Valley really tells you how futile the whole thing is. The biggest ground in London and there was no one there. No one at all. Terrible. Still we won another £2 (less tax). And I made the winner with a great through ball to Derek Smethurst.

The first team are playing Luton tomorrow in the League Cup at the Den. Even though I want to get away, I feel really sick missing it. You feel so out of it, so useless. I couldn't go and watch tomorrow.

24 November

Millwall 0   Orient 1

I went to Walton and Hersham for LBC to watch their Cup match against Brighton. LBC want me to get an interview with Clough for them. Which I am quite keen to do. I don't know about him. I wrote an article in my weekly column about him and Allison, making a contrast between them and the grey men who rule in many clubs. The people who never try to change the game, who never speak out about the bad things in the game, but are always willing to knock Clough and Allison, and who are delighted now they are both struggling. Benny is delighted. He is saying 'Now they are getting their come-uppance. This is good for the game, because they are bad for it.'

When we got back to the studio, the LBC reporter at Millwall's game had brought a copy of their programme back with him. And inside was an editorial attacking me for my column about Clough and Allison. So it looks as if Benny has finally decided to give into my pressure and let me go. The article said:

No doubt many Millwall supporters and not a few *South London Press* readers, who know of Millwall but are not supporters, are puzzled by the weekly article which appears in that journal under the heading of 'Dunphy's Diary'. Of course, if you happen to know Eamon and his philosophy you will appreciate his attitude to the established order of life. Obviously, if you have not already recognized the fact, Eamon is opposed to the establishment, football or otherwise. Deep down in all of us there resides this spirit of rebellion, but if we all rebelled, if we all took up the cudgels in support of a complete revolution of the present order of things, there would be only one result – CHAOS. The latest diatribe from Dunphy finds him supporting the ideas and ideals of those paramount rebels of soccer society, Malcolm Allison and Brian Clough. Fair enough, we are all entitled to our opinion and Eamon has frankly confessed his. He is opposed to what he calls 'the little men'. Now we have never doubted that people like Eamon suffer from a lack of intelligence, but when he begins to describe people who have given a life-time to the game, and provided brains and finance to ensure its continuance, as 'little', then it is about time he got his priorities right. In football today there are men and that includes managers, who, don't forget, were at some time in their careers on the same side of the fence as Eamon, who have unselfishly given the game the benefit of business experience and the kind of financial backing which in the normal way would be considered foolish ventures, to provide a living for such as Eamon Dunphy. We don't decry the outbursts, the egotistical expositions of people like Malcolm Allison, Brian Clough and those like Eamon who follow in their wake, because after all it is just a question of 'blowing one's top'. The 'faceless ones' so carelessly referred to by Eamon help him to keep the wolf from the door. Is it so wrong to try and keep the game on an even keel? Is it wrong to keep a level-headed approach to a situation which requires everyone concerned with its survival to behave unselfishly, and believe you me that is not bringing the wolf to the door for those who seek to change things (we would all like the kind of money Malcolm Allison, Brian Clough and to a degree Eamon Dunphy pick up). Is it ideals which inspire this blowing of one's top? If history is any guide, most idealists existed in poverty. Today's so-called idealists, by virtue of the communications media, get paid for their outbursts. They also get paid for remaining loyal to those who provide them with a living, a very good living at that. We could all blow our top. The writer of the article for instance, but, to repeat an old adage of ours, the game is greater than those who seek most to gain from it. The game goes on. You change it by the process of ordered thought, not by outbursts which boost your own ego, which give you a headline in a local or national paper. Far too many people in the game today are persuaded by personal publicity to boost the circulation of newspapers. If Malcolm Allison, Brian Clough and to a lesser degree Eamon Dunphy say it, then must it be believed? We have said it before and we don't blush when we say it again. Make your own minds up.

26 November

I was sitting at home this evening when the phone went. It was Theo Foley, the Charlton manager, and an old team-mate from the Irish team. He was at the Hilton at a boxing dinner. 'What is the problem at Millwall?' I told him that I wanted to get away.

'Well,' he said, 'I had a chat with Benny this afternoon, and he is willing to let you go. I can't understand it, because when I came for you last year, he wouldn't hear of it. What is the story? Have you lost interest in the game? Don't you want to play any more? Because he tells me he is sick of you.'

'No, I haven't lost interest in the game. On the contrary I want to go on and try to achieve something. I still want to play.'

'Well,' said Theo, 'I'm still interested. I still want you to come, subject to having a chat with you, finding out your thing. Benny has given me permission to approach you. Don't say anything when you go in in the morning. He will call you into the office and tell you, and then you can come over and have a chat. If you are interested in joining us, we will see what we can do.'

I'm both excited and frightened by the thought. I've wanted a move for so long. I told Sandra, and she said 'You don't want to go to a Third Division club.' I said 'What the hell, it's a club. You can play, you can start afresh, you can find out how good you are or how bad you are without any of the prejudices that exist after eight years at one place.'

I was really excited by the idea. I think I would have been excited if it had been Stevenage Town. Because it means someone wants you, someone thinks you can do a job for them. I think players are still excited and gratified by the fact that some manager somewhere thinks that you can do a job for him.

There is no way going to the Third Division should excite anyone. But it is exciting. And frightening. Because I'm not an adventurer. I've been at Millwall for eight years. I like stability and security. But I know I will go if I have half a chance.

27 November

I did just as Theo said. I went to the ground this morning, and I didn't say a word to anybody. I got my kit on, and I was just pulling my jockstrap on when Jack came down and said 'Benny wants to see you in his office.'

So I finished getting changed and went up to the office. We weren't too friendly now, because of the rows and ructions, but there was some preliminary small talk. Then he said 'I've fixed you up a nice little move if you want to. Just down the road at Charlton.' I feigned surprise and said yes, I would be interested in talking to them. 'Right,' he said. 'Theo wants you to go over there now and have a chat with him.'

'I don't want you to leave,' he said. 'There is a place for you here as long as I'm here. But you've put me in a position where it is as easy for me to sell you as it is to keep you. Do you want to go and have a chat to him?'

'Yes!' I said.

After I had changed, I went back up to the office to phone for a taxi. 'I'll run you over,' said Benny.

On the way over I was frightened to death. Really excited. My hands were all sweaty with the excitement. I suppose it is only a simple move, but I felt really nervous. We got as far as Charlton Vale, and Benny stopped the car.

'Look,' he said, 'you know I've never done you any harm. I've only tried to do the best for you. We've had our differences, but as long as you want to stay at Millwall there's a place for you. I'll give you a testimonial. You've only got two years to do, so you should think about that. I can't guarantee you a first-team place, nobody can, but I want you to stay. This could be a disastrous move for you, and it could be disastrous for me. Before you go in there, I'm telling you, don't sign anything until you come back and see me.'

So I went into the ground. It is funny, but I've never liked Charlton. There has never seemed any soul there, no guts, no atmosphere. As a team they always seemed like a nice load of nancy boys. We've always loved playing against them, because we've never had a game against them. It's been too easy.

But they want me. It is a challenge, which is very clichéd, but is important. I think that if I can get away from Millwall, get away from the past, and start playing on my own merits, without any prejudices, I can do a good job for somebody.

I went in. I had decided to go there before I saw Theo. But I went up to see him.

'What have you been doing to Benny?'

'Nothing. I just put a bit of pressure on to get away.'

So Theo went over the same story he had told me last night, about meeting Benny at some function, and Benny saying he was sick of me. And he asked me if I wanted to play, or was just eager to find a nice resting place to mess about for a couple of years. So I assured him that I wanted to achieve something in the game, I was still ambitious and all the rest of it. And he said he had seen me in the reserves at Orient, and been impressed with the way I had worked. Which was funny, because that had been a day when I had really had to gee myself up. Then he told me what he hoped, and what he thought his team could do. He said that they needed someone in midfield who could gee people up, have a bit of enthusiasm for the game, and give a bit of leadership.

Which was all very nice. Then we discussed wages. Your club always tells the other club what your current salary is to give them a guideline. I wasn't too worried about the money. Providing it was adequate. They offered a fiver a week more than Millwall, which was OK. But then we had to negotiate a signing-on fee or loyalty bonus, because I was losing the testominial I would have got from Millwall if I stayed.

The signing-on fee is crucial in football these days. All sorts of stories fly around the game about X and Y and Z. 'Did you hear about him? He went there and he got £7,000 in his hand.' In the Third Division that is too. I've never had any of it.

So I said to Theo 'I want to discuss a loyalty bonus. But first I must go back to Millwall and see about getting my house.'

He said 'We've got a club house.' And we went and had a look. It was terrible. A real slum. And I got very worried because it had suddenly dawned on me that I am living in a Millwall house, and that this house which I regard as my own is really not mine at all. It is tied completely to where I am and what I do. And it suddenly hit me, and I really got frightened. It struck me that I'm not independent at all, even though I've always liked to think that I am. I haven't got anywhere to live. I'm living in a grace-and-favour house.

I really felt disturbed. I had always felt this house was my right. And it wasn't. I felt really vulnerable. I've got nothing. No money, no security, no trade, no home. Only my skills. So I thought 'I've got to get a home.' And I went back to Millwall determined to try to get Millwall to sell it to me, and to get enough from Charlton to buy it. And all I had to bargain with was my own little bit of skill, which really, when you compare it with a carpenter's skill, or a plumber's skill, is intangible. They can make chairs, or mend the loo. But a footballer? A Second or Third Division footballer is expendable. You can easily be done without.

So I went back to see Benny. He was not very receptive initially. But I persuaded him that he had had eight years out of me, and I had nothing to show for it. That they weren't having to give me a testimonial, which I would be entitled to soon, and were making a profit on my sale. And finally he agreed.

So I rang Theo, and he took me out to dinner. We went to Blackheath Steak House. And agreed terms. But he told me not to say anything, because the Charlton chairman is in hospital, and Theo wants to see him before he reads it in the papers. I suppose Theo is frightened that if he reads that they have signed that well-known rebel Dunphy, he might have a relapse.

So I am delighted. Peter Ball phoned, and I told him. 'Why Charlton?' he said. 'Surely there are better places you could go?'

But they want me. I like Theo, he is an excellent coach, they have got some good youngsters, and they want me. And I want to go somewhere where I can feel useful and wanted. Not stay part of a set-up I don't believe in any more.

28 November

I signed for Charlton today.

I went to the Den to pick up my boots. The lads were out training so I did not see anyone to say good-bye. I could not have faced it anyway. I had spent a long time there wanting to get away, but now that the time came, I wondered if I was doing the right thing. Not rationally. Rationally I knew it was right. But I had spent a long time there, and I feel a lot of affection for the place. It is a unique place, a unique club. And a great bunch of lads: Alan, Kitch, Harry, Gordon Bolland, Alfie. There are few clubs with such fine characters.

But rationally I knew I had done the right thing. I had no part to play there any more. Our team had broken up. I know I would get back in if I stayed, but to what end? Dennis has gone already. Harry is out, Franky is ignored, Gordon is out. Alfie is desperate to get away. In three months the team which I hoped, we all hoped, would see us in the First Division has been broken up. And the 'new side' has taken over.

They have had a few good results, although they lost on Saturday. They are in with a good chance of getting somewhere in the League Cup. But I don't believe they have got the necessary character to do it. I think Benny has got a team which will just lead him into trouble, possibly even get him sacked. When I said that to him a couple of weeks ago, he said 'Results have proved you wrong, son.' We will see. I hope in a way that I am wrong, because I would hate to see Benny sacked. I think he has been wrong to make these changes, but I like him in spite of all our disagreements.

I hope that Charlton will be different, that it will be somewhere where the set-up is right. Because that is the most important thing. It is like a rose. In good soil they bloom; on stony ground they don't. And footballers are the same. At Millwall we had the players, the character, the desire and the skill. But the set-up was wrong.

A Journalist's View
(Peter Ball)

At one stage this book was conceived as telling the same story from three different perspectives: player's, fan's and journalist's. This report was part of Peter Ball's proposed contribution. It is included because it illustrates fairly dramatically the contrast between the professional and the outsider's views, in particular in the post mortem held by Eamon and Peter Ball.

Millwall 1   Sheffield Wednesday 0

It was my first visit of the season to the Den. Millwall were without Denny Burnett and Dougy Allder from the team I'd seen last season. And instead of a flash little winger in Stevie Brown, they had another flash little winger in Gordon Hill. On the evidence of this game, I reckon Stevie's tactic of getting to the flag and crossing was more useful than Hill's attempts to go it alone. The addition of another big boy in Brian Clark, which sent Gordon Bolland wide on the right, added further power up front. But in retrospect it seems to have lessened their options.

At least that's what the game suggested. Sure, it was an exciting game. In the first ten minutes Millwall attacked furiously. A couple of headers from Wood and Clark nearly went in. But then, gradually, you began to notice that Wednesday were the more poised side. Craig had the control and authority in midfield which Millwall without Burnett lacked. Saul, his replacement, ran around a lot. Wednesday twice broke fast and well. The first time a delayed pass put Knighton offside. The second time Prendergast was set completely free on the right, Cripps presumably was still trying desperately to meet up with Potts, Wednesday's replacement for Willie Henderson. Prendergast shot hurriedly and high.

Then on the twenty-minute mark Millwall put together their first and only real movement of the night. All along the ground from left back to the right corner flag, where Bolland sent over a cross. Again Wood got his head to it. This time Springett saved for a corner. At last – five or six passes put together along the ground going forward. At last. But the corner was cleared and Wednesday continued to play cool, unhurried and skilful football. And the more they remained poised, the more Millwall struggled. The more they struggled, the more frantic their play became. At half-time it was o–o. But Wednesday looked the likelier to break the deadlock.

In the second half Millwall charged forward again. For a time Wednesday reeled. But they still kept cool. With twenty or twenty-five minutes to go, it seemed inevitable that they would win. But slowly, caution overcame them. Instead of driving forward, exploiting their superior ability, they began to think about the point in their possession. So their attacks became half-hearted. And bad finishing finished them. Around the eightieth minute they were twice in a goalscoring position, and twice they fluffed it. Once when a brilliant move had left the defence nowhere, Dunphy sprinted thirty yards to make a last-ditch tackle.

The game stayed poised. Balanced between guts, or character or whatever you want to call it, on the one hand, and superior skill and poise on the other. So perhaps a draw was going to be a fair result. Wednesday for the last ten minutes looked to have settled for a draw. Millwall urged themselves forward for that last onslaught, but it was always desperation. Wednesday still looked self-contained. But with three or four minutes to go, Wednesday's attack, which was now down to one man, broke again. And they sustained it. Which drew them forward. It would be interesting to know their psychology at that stage. Had they settled for a draw with ten minutes to go, but their inherent footballing ability kept on asserting itself against safety-first tactics? Did they realize they were the better side and that a bit more assertion would give them two points? Or was it just carelessness? Anyway, for a throw-in near Millwall's corner flag, Wednesday were up. Millwall won the ball, moved it quickly and sent it over the heads of the defence for Gordon Hill to chase. But it didn't get there. Peter Rodrigues jumped and pulled it down with his hands, getting booked and giving Millwall a free kick fifteen yards inside the Wednesday half. Dunphy took the kick. One of his perfectly placed kicks. And there was Alf Wood meeting it and hitting the back of the net. Everyone swarmed to Wood except Dunphy, who reacted like an exulting mahdi. Racing back to the half-way line both fists clenched and falling on his knees. To say he looked like someone who had just seen God would be wrong. He had. The other players reached him to add their congratulations and he leaped into the arms of Alf Wood, still exulting, still with fists clenched. 1–0. Ninety seconds later the whistle went.

The next morning the papers talked about Rodrigues's moment of aberration. If it hadn't produced a goal it would have either gone unmentioned, or been dismissed as a piece of professionalism. Panic or calculation? I don't know which it was. Real calculation would have let Gordon Hill have that ball. He'd flashed around during the game, but had always dribbled himself into trouble. And although he was fast and would have had a couple of yards on Rodrigues, he had to go wide to collect the ball, and that would have given Rodrigues time to get between him and the area. If it was cynicism then it was out of character with the way Wednesday had played. Not that Wednesday would blame Rodrigues. The footballers' culprit would be the man who failed to pick up Wood.

But those considerations were for later. The goal went in, and we all leaped up. Eamon had a lot of people in the stand that night. We all met and went up to the players' room. And they were all saying 'Great, wasn't that great?' And I went and talked to Billy Neill. After pleasantries he asked me what I thought. And I said 'Well, the boys did well. It was a good game, but I thought the better side lost.'

'Aye,' said Billy. 'They were a good side, Wednesday. Played the better football.'

We talked about how they had been cool and composed, where Millwall were desperate and struggling to find their touch. And what a superb player Craig was. And Billy said he'd been sitting with Johnny Sissons, who'd said that they all got on to Craig at Wednesday because he sent out great balls, and then stood and admired them instead of carrying on moving. I'd said I'd not noticed that, but what great balls he sent out. Which Billy agreed with. And we said that maybe, now that Millwall had beaten Wednesday, who were such a good side, it would give them the confidence to settle and play football without the tinge of desperation. And then Billy went down to the changing-room.

That was all interesting. The comments over Craig showed the split between the way footballers see players – and of course the game – and the way anyone else sees it. We can accept flaws in exchange for the flair, the moment of vision or artistry. Footballers see the flaws. But the conversation also showed, I thought for a little while, that I wasn't far off in my judgements. Billy and I had agreed about the game, and about both teams in the game. So I was then able to go and listen to everyone saying 'Great, wasn't that great?'

In a way, of course, it was. Millwall had had slightly the worse of a top-class game. They had had a bad run, and were desperate. Consequently Wednesday showed up as the better football side. Possibly, as I'd said to Billy Neill, this win was just what they needed to give them a bit of confidence. Then they could settle and play football instead of the freneticism which they had shown tonight. Eamon could stop running around like a madman trying to do the work of three, and get back to doing his own job properly. Adding a bit of cool and insight and subtlety. If the win itself had set them up to play the football they can (or have I been conned into believing they can by Eamon's faith?), then it was great. And it was great because in the famous motto, if you win when you're not playing well, then you are a good side.

But that wasn't why everyone else was saying 'Great.' That was because they had not seen it the way I had. They had come to watch Millwall, and Eamon in particular. And fate had decreed that after a lot of struggle, Eamon had set up the winning goal. And so it was great. They certainly weren't thinking of Wednesday, as I was. Thinking what a good side, thinking how they had deserved a point, at least. Hoping that yet another away defeat wouldn't start fear and negativity appearing more noticeably when they came away. Hoping that the commitment both sides had shown in tackles wouldn't be changed into something more brutal and cynical. Hoping that they would think 'If we'd been a bit more positive we'd have won that game' rather than 'If we'd been a bit more cautious we'd have got a point.'

And then Eamon appeared. Bubbling. Going around happily to everyone. 'Great, wasn't it great?' When he came over to me, he said 'Character. That is what it's about.' And I said 'Yeah. It was a good game, and a good win for you. But the better side lost.' He looked at me in total disbelief for a moment. Then 'Bloody journalists.' Another moment's silence. 'How can you say that? They played it around a bit. But the pressure was on us. And we accepted it and kept going longer than they did. And that is what it is all about. Character. If was bloody hard out there. They weren't giving anything away. And we pressured them and they cracked.'

And I said 'The better side lost. Ask Billy Neill. He agreed with that. It's not just journalist's talk.'

'Billy Neill said that?' And Eamon turned and went to talk to somebody else. Someone who could accept what he had seen.

And that was it until we were all sitting in the restaurant having supper. The wine flowed, and we talked about politics and women's lib and whatever. Then Eamon suddenly attacked. For some reason Manchester United came up, and he proposed a toast to the only Manchester United fan remaining – me. All good-humoured. But then for a few moments it wasn't. You don't, unless you're very close to him, tell a footballer he had a bad game, or his team didn't deserve to win. Not until the euphoria has died down anyway.

Eamon was hurt. And for a few minutes, it all came out. In an attack. 'Why do you always like losers? Manchester United, West Ham, tonight.' It was an unfair attack. Eamon knew that too. He knew that if I didn't despise West Ham as much as he did, they were far from being a team I admired. But my parry on that was dismissed, and we returned to tonight. And went over the same ground. Character, courage, work. That it was really hard, and when you weren't getting the results you could either react by working yourself stupid, as Millwall had done, or you could ponce around, or you could just hide. But they'd kept going and pressurized and worked and in the end had got their reward. Because they had had the character, Wednesday hadn't. So Wednesday cracked in the end.

And I said perhaps that was right. But if so, where did that place their results against Blackpool and Preston? Hadn't they cracked in the end? Didn't that mean that Millwall's much-vaunted character was possessed even more strongly by Blackpool and Preston? Or wasn't it a nonsense word anyway? And that what I'd said was that Wednesday that night were the better team. Maybe they *had* been in a situation where they could afford to be cool, and play it around, because the onus to be positive was on Millwall. But it hadn't been an Aston Villa 'professional performance' with eight men back all the time and ten back most. And I said that anyway I hadn't said Wednesday deserved to win, but that they were marginally the better side on the night, and a draw would have been a fair result on the night. And that maybe Millwall could outplay them. But that at the moment they lacked confidence, and were struggling a bit. And as a result their play became frantic. That what they really needed was someone to give them a bit of the calm and precision Wednesday had. Which perhaps the return of Burnett would bring. To which Eamon said Saul had played well, although he half-heartedly accepted the rest.

But again the disagreement over Saul was crucial. Saul had run around a lot, and had worked very hard. As had Eamon. But most of the time Millwall's midfield were challenging for Wednesday's ball, rather than having their own to start attacks with. So they had to run around a lot. But when they did get the ball, haste was uppermost. Saul couldn't and Eamon wouldn't keep possession and look for the telling pass like Craig did for Wednesday. Whenever a Wednesday defender got the ball, their midfield players found space, and the ball was channelled to them to organize things. But Eamon and Saul chased back to defend and then chased up after the ball was booted away for one of the front-runners. Panic. Or, if that's too strong a word, pressure. But it was the difference between a good-looking team who carved out three or four real chances and always looked purposeful, and a side who were getting by on effort and determination.

Allowing for Millwall's bad start, it was two good points and a useful morale-booster. But unless it paved the way for more cool football, then hopes for the top three were a chimera.

First-Team Results, 1973-4

Given below is a complete list of first-team results, comprising League Division Two, FA Cup and Football League Cup fixtures. The results are given in date order, with the full Millwall team and the Millwall goalscorers.

25 August

Fulham 2   Millwall 0

King, Brown B., Cripps, Dorney, Kitchener, Burnett, Brown S. (Wainwright), Bolland, Wood, Dunphy, Allder

1 September

Millwall 1 (Wood)   Aston Villa 1

King, Brown B., Cripps, Dorney, Kitchener, Burnett, Bolland, Clark, Wood, Dunphy, Allder

8 September

Blackpool 1   Millwall 0

King, Brown B., Cripps, Dorney, Kitchener, Bolland, Saul, Clark, Wood, Dunphy, Hill

11 September

Preston N.E. 2   Millwall 0

King, Brown B., Cripps, Dorney, Kitchener, Saul, Clark (Wainwright), Bolland, Wood, Dunphy, Hill

15 September

Millwall 3 (Clark, Wood, Bolland)   Hull C. 0

King ,Brown B., Cripps, Dorney, Kitchener, Bolland, Saul, Clark, Wood, Dunphy, Hill

17 September

Millwall 1 (Wood)   Sheffield W. 0

King, Brown B., Cripps, Dorney, Kitchener, Saul, Bolland, Clark, Wood, Dunphy, Hill

22 September

Swindon T. 1   Millwall 3 (Bolland 2, Clark)

King, Brown B., Cripps, Dorney, Kitchener, Saul, Bolland, Clark, Wood, Dunphy, Hill

29 September

Millwall 1 (Bolland)   Carlisle U. 2

King, Brown B., Cripps, Dorney, Kitchener, Bolland, Saul, Clark, Wood, Dunphy, Hill

3 October

Sheffield W. 3   Millwall 2 (Wood 2)

King, Brown B., Cripps, Dorney, Kitchener, Burnett, Bolland (Hill), Wainwright, Clark, Wood, Saul

6 October

Nottingham F. 3   Millwall 0

King, Brown B., Cripps, Dorney, Kitchener, Burnett, Bolland, Wainwright, Clark, Wood, Saul

10 October   Football League Cup, 2nd Round

Millwall 0   Nottingham F. 0

King, Brown B., Cripps, Dorney, Kitchener, Burnett, Bolland, Clark, Wood, Dunphy, Hill

13 October

Millwall 0   Bristol C. 2

King, Brown B., Cripps, Dorney, Kitchener, Burnett, Bolland, Clark, Wood, Dunphy, Hill

16 October   Football League Cup, 2nd Round (Replay)

Nottingham F. 1   Millwall 3 (Clark, Hill, Brown S.)

King, Donaldson, Jones, Dorney, Kitchener, Burnett, Brown S., Clark, Wood, Dunphy, Hill

20 October

Bolton W. 0   Millwall 1 (Clark)

King, Jones, Donaldson, Dorney, Kitchener, Burnett, Brown S., Clark, Wood, Dunphy, Hill

22 October

Millwall 5 (Wood 3, Clark, McNab [o.g.])   Preston N.E. 1

King, Donaldson, Jones, Dorney, Kitchener, Burnett, Brown S., Clark, Wood, Dunphy, Hill

27 October

Millwall 0   Middlesbrough 1

King, Donaldson, Jones, Dorney, Kitchener, Burnett, Brown S., Clark, Wood, Dunphy (Bolland), Hill

31 October   Football League Cup, 3rd Round

Millwall 1 (Clark)   Bolton W. 1

Sherwood, Donaldson, Jones, Dorney, Kitchener, Allder, Brown S., Kelly, Wood, Clark, Hill

3 November

Notts C. 3   Millwall 3 (Allder [pen.], Kelly, Hill)

Sherwood, Donaldson, Jones, Dorney, Kitchener, Kelly, Brown S., Clark, Wood, Allder, Hill

6 November   Football League Cup, 3rd Round (Replay)

Bolton W. 1   Millwall 2 (McAllister [o.g.], Wood)

King, Donaldson, Jones, Dorney, Kitchener, Allder, Brown S., Kelly, Wood, Clark, Hill

10 November

Millwall 2 (Wood, Hill)   Cardiff C. 0

King, Donaldson, Jones, Dorney, Kitchener, Allder, Brown S., Clark, Wood (Brown B.), Kelly, Hill

17 November

C. Palace 1   Millwall 1 (Bolland)

King, Donaldson, Jones, Dorney, Kitchener, Allder, Bolland, Kelly, Wood, Clark, Hill

21 November   Football League Cup, 4th Round

Millwall 3 (Allder, Kelly, Clark)   Luton T. 1 (Jones [o.g.])

King, Donaldson, Jones, Dorney, Kitchener, Allder, Bolland, Kelly, Wood, Clark, Hill (Brown S.)

24 November

Millwall 0   Orient 1

King, Donaldson, Jones, Dorney, Kitchener, Allder, Brown S., Kelly, Wood (Bolland), Clark, Hill

8 December

Millwall 0   Luton T. 1

King, Donaldson, Jones, Dorney, Kitchener, Allder, Brown S. (Bolland), Clark, Wood, Kelly, Hill

15 December

Millwall 2 (Wood, Hill)   Sunderland 1

King, Donaldson, Jones, Dorney, Kitchener, Allder, Saul, Clark, Wood, Bolland, Hill

19 December   Football League Cup, 5th Round

Millwall 1 (Wood)   Norwich 1

King, Donaldson, Jones, Dorney, Kitchener, Allder, Bolland, Clark, Wood, Saul, Hill

22 December

Carlisle U. 1   Millwall 1 (Wood)

King, Donaldson, Jones, Dorney, Kitchener, Allder (Kelly), Saul, Clark, Wood, Bolland, Hill

26 December

Millwall 1 (Wood)   Portsmouth 1

King, Donaldson, Jones, Dorney, Kitchener, Allder, Bolland, Clark, Wood, Saul, Hill

29 December

Millwall 2 (Wood, Clark)   Blackpool 2

King, Jones, Donaldson, Dorney, Kitchener, Allder, Bolland, Clark, Wood, Saul, Hill

1 January

Aston Villa 0   Millwall 0

King, Donaldson, Jones, Dorney, Kitchener, Allder, Bolland, Clark, Wood, Saul, Hill

5 January   FA Cup, 3rd Round

Millwall 1 (Wood)   Scunthorpe U. 1

King, Brown B., Jones, Donaldson, Dorney, Allder, Bolland, Clark, Wood, Saul (Smethurst), Hill

8 January   FA Cup, 3rd Round (Replay)

Scunthorpe U. 1   Millwall 0

King, Brown B., Jones, Donaldson, Dorney, Allder, Bolland, Clark, Wood, Smethurst, Hill

12 January

Hull C. 1   Millwall 1 (Smethurst)

King, Donaldson, Jones, Dorney, Kitchener, Allder, Bolland, Clark, Wood, Smethurst, Hill

16 January   Football League Cup, 5th Round (Replay)

Norwich 2   Millwall 1 (Smethurst)

King, Donaldson, Jones, Dorney, Kitchener, Allder, Bolland, Clark, Wood, Smethurst, Hill

20 January

Millwall 1 (Clark)   Fulham 0

King, Donaldson, Jones, Dorney, Kitchener, Allder, Bolland, Clark, Wood, Smethurst, Hill

26 January

Oxford U. 0   Millwall 3 (Hill 2, Clark)

King, Donaldson, Jones, Dorney, Kitchener, Allder, Bolland, Clark, Wood, Smethurst, Hill

2 February

Sunderland 4   Millwall 0

King, Donaldson, Jones, Dorney, Kitchener, Allder, Bolland, Clark, Wood, Smethurst, Hill

16 February

Millwall 3 (Bolland [pen.], Wood 2)   Swindon T. 0

King, Donaldson, Jones, Dorney, Kitchener, Allder, Bolland, Clark, Wood, Smethurst, Hill

23 February

Millwall 0   Nottingham F. 0

King, Donaldson, Jones, Dorney, Kitchener, Allder, Bolland, Clark, Wood, Smethurst, Hill

26 February

Bristol C. 5   Millwall 2 (Smethurst, Hill)

King, Brown B., Jones, Dorney, Kitchener, Allder, Bolland, Clark, Wood, Smethurst, Hill

2 March

Portsmouth o   Millwall o

King, Brown B., Cripps, Dorney, Kitchener, Allder, Bolland, Clark, Wood, Smethurst, Hill

9 March

Middlesbrough 2   Millwall 1 (Clark)

King, Donaldson, Cripps, Dorney, Kitchener, Allder, Saul, Clark, Wood, Smethurst, Hill

16 March

Millwall 2 (Wood, Smethurst)   Bolton W. 1

King, Jones, Cripps, Dorney, Kitchener, Allder, Saul, Clark, Wood, Smethurst, Hill

23 March

Cardiff C. 1   Millwall 3 (Cripps, Clark, Hill)

King, Donaldson, Cripps, Dorney, Kitchener, Allder, Saul, Clark, Wood, Smethurst (Bolland), Hill

30 March

Millwall o   Notts Co. o

King, Donaldson, Cripps, Dorney, Kitchener, Allder, Saul, Clark, Wood, Smethurst, Hill

6 April

Orient 1   Millwall 1 (Wood)

King, Donaldson, Cripps, Dorney, Kitchener, Allder, Saul, Clark, Wood, Smethurst, Hill

12 April

Millwall 1 (Wood [pen.]) W.B.A. 0

King, Donaldson, Cripps, Dorney, Kitchener, Allder, Saul, Clark, Wood, Smethurst, Hill

13 April

Millwall 3 (Clark, Wood 2) C. Palace 2

King, Donaldson, Cripps, Dorney, Kitchener, Allder, Saul, Clark, Wood, Smethurst, Hill

17 April

W.B.A. 1 Millwall 1 (Wood)

King, Jones, Cripps, Dorney, Kitchener, Allder, Saul, Clark, Wood, Smethurst, Hill

20 April

Luton T. 3 Millwall 0

King, Jones, Cripps, Dorney, Kitchener, Allder, Saul, Clark, Wood, Smethurst, Hill

27 April

Millwall 0 Oxford U. 0

King, Jones, Cripps, Donaldson, Dorney, Allder, Saul, Clark, Wood, Smethurst, Hill

The Final League Division Two Table, 1973–4

	P	Home					Away					Pts
		W	D	L	F	A	W	D	L	F	A	
Middlesbrough	42	16	4	1	40	8	11	7	3	37	22	65
Luton T.	42	12	5	4	42	25	7	7	7	22	26	50
Carlisle U.	42	13	5	3	40	17	7	4	10	21	31	49
Orient	42	9	8	4	28	17	6	10	5	27	25	48
Blackpool	42	11	5	5	35	17	6	8	7	22	23	47
Sunderland	42	11	6	4	32	15	8	3	10	26	29	47
Nottingham F.	42	12	6	3	40	19	3	9	9	17	24	45
W.B.A.	42	8	9	4	28	24	6	7	8	20	21	44
Hull C.	42	9	9	3	25	15	4	8	9	21	32	43
Notts Co.	42	8	6	7	30	35	7	7	7	25	25	43
Bolton W.	42	12	5	4	30	17	3	7	11	14	23	42
Millwall	42	10	6	5	28	16	4	8	9	23	35	42
Fulham	42	11	4	6	26	20	5	6	10	13	23	42
Aston Villa	42	8	9	4	33	21	5	6	10	15	24	41
Portsmouth	42	9	8	4	26	16	5	4	12	19	46	40
Bristol C.	42	9	5	7	25	20	5	5	11	22	34	38
Cardiff C.	42	8	7	6	27	20	2	9	10	22	42	36
Oxford U.	42	8	8	5	27	21	2	8	11	8	25	36
Sheffield W.	42	9	6	6	33	24	3	5	13	18	39	35
C. Palace	42	6	7	8	24	24	5	5	11	19	32	34
Preston N.E.	42	7	8	6	24	23	2	6	13	16	39	31
Swindon T.	42	6	7	8	22	27	1	4	16	14	45	25

Postscript (1986)
by Peter Ball

Eamon

Perhaps predictably, his time at Millwall was to prove the high point of Eamon's playing career, although he was to help both Charlton and Reading to promotion before he retired. The move to Charlton was not immediately successful. In his desperate desire to justify Theo Foley's belief in him, he was too involved, too committed, trying to take too much responsibility and do other players' jobs, and, inevitably, his own game suffered. The side failed to make good their challenge for promotion and Theo Foley was sacked at the end of the season.

Foley was replaced by Andy Nelson. Eamon suspected that he was not Nelson's type of player, but although he was sidelined for spells with a back injury – a problem which was to recur until a major operation in 1985 promised to solve it – he played his part in the side gaining promotion. He played in the first three of their last four games, when promotion nerves were taking hold as they tried to gather the last few points necessary, scoring a vital goal at Hereford to get a draw. The team lost the penultimate match at Chesterfield, however, and he was dropped for the final, promotion-winning game against Preston. And he was given a free transfer.

He then moved to Reading, and although he was hampered by back trouble, he played an influential part in their promotion to the

Third Division in his first season, 1975–6. As so often happens, however, success brought its own problems: the players felt that they were not rewarded adequately and the discontent was reflected on the field the following year as they failed to consolidate their position in the Third Division. Eamon, not surprisingly, had been one of the players' spokesmen, and although he and others thought he was playing as well as ever, he was given a free transfer at the end of the season. It was the end of his playing career.

Initially, he hoped to stay in the game. In his last season at Reading he coached London University, taking them to third place in the B U S F tournament, their highest ranking for a decade – a considerable achievement with a willing but generally limited group of players. That success and the very high mark he achieved on his F A coaching course – something which made him rethink his dismissive views of the coaching establishment – strengthened his conviction that he had a lot to offer as a manager, and he began to apply for vacancies.

The mediocrities who run most English Football League clubs, however, did not agree. Workington did not even bother to reply to his application; they went on to lose their Football League place at the end of that season. Others were more polite but no more encouraging, providing another example of English football having no use for its brightest and best graduates.

John Giles turned his back on English football at the same time, moving back to Dublin to take over Shamrock Rovers. After an unavailing search for work in England, Eamon joined him, becoming youth team coach, a post he also filled for the international team.

While at Reading, he had begun to develop his writing, contributing a weekly column to the local paper which was much admired, and the move to Dublin brought greater opportunities in that area. In his early years he had been too influenced by 'great writers' and in consequence his own writing often seemed stilted, but a sympathetic sub-editor on the *Irish Times* got the message across that genuine Dunphy was far preferable to *ersatz* Shaw or Sheridan, and a series of brilliant articles on the 1978 World Cup signified that a new career was always available if he wanted it.

Readers of his diary will not be surprised to learn that initially he resisted the idea. Giles's dream of building a great European club in Dublin did not translate into reality, however, and Eamon's frustration grew. Eventually, he left Shamrock Rovers to devote himself to journalism, although he retained his post with Ireland until the incompatibility of working for the FAI and writing about his country's footballing failures became apparent.

He made only one attempt to get back into the game. He had always harboured the dream of managing Millwall and building them into a powerful force, and although he was settled in Dublin he was persuaded to let his name be put forward by the late Herbert Burnige when Peter Anderson was sacked in 1982. Burnige's support, however, failed to sway the new chairman, Alan Thorne, who preferred the claims of George Graham, and with that rebuff he closed the book on his footballing ambitions.

His writing, however, has been an unqualified success. It will surprise no one to learn that he has proved himself a brilliant, incisive and provocative sports journalist, making a major contribution to the success of the new quality Irish Sunday paper, the *Sunday Tribune*. At the risk of being accused of bias, I would say that he has set new standards for football writing in the British Isles; there is certainly not a paper in Britain whose football coverage would not be strengthened by his presence. His writing has also led him into new areas. His TV criticism for the *Sunday Tribune* has been exceptional, and his political interests prompted him to act as a speech-writer for Fine Gael ministers during the 1982 elections, although perhaps sensibly he rejected suggestions that he should stand for election with the view to becoming Minister of Sport.

As that suggests, his political allegiances have changed from his days as a socialist in the early seventies, but his hunger for intellectual stimulation is unabated and so too is his volatile temperament. At the beginning of 1986 he changed tack again, resigning from the *Sunday Tribune* after a series of disagreements with its equally unyielding editor, Vincent Browne, to work as a freelance. Wherever he is, he will undoubtedly continue to make waves.

Millwall

Twelve years, four managers and three chairmen later, Millwall are in much the same position as they were when Eamon left, sitting in the lower middle of the Second Division. It is safe to conclude that they have not made progress in the intervening period, but that bald statement disguises some eventful times.

As Eamon predicted, and feared, Benny's new team was one to get him the sack. Benny survived less than twelve months after Eamon's departure. The team successfully negotiated the rest of the 1973–4 season in mid-table but began the following campaign badly. In late September they were in twenty-first place, and a boardroom coup took place, Herbert Burnige replacing Mickey Purser. It was the end for Benny Fenton and he was replaced by Gordon Jago.

Jago's arrival was followed by wholesale changes on and off the field. Much influenced by American marketing ideas, Jago set out to change the image of the club. The Den was painted, the cold visiting team's dressing-room was made more welcoming and he even attempted to persuade the local council to change the address from Cold Blow Lane to Montego Bay Avenue. That was unsuccessful, and initially Jago's far-reaching changes in personnel were equally so, the club being relegated in his first season. They came straight back up, but after one season of successful consolidation they began the 1977–8 season badly and Jago left at Christmas to move to America with Tampa Bay Rowdies. Theo Foley, who had joined Millwall as Jago's assistant, took over temporarily but it was George Petchey who was given the job of avoiding relegation.

That season he was successful, but by then the club's increasingly bad reputation for crowd trouble had received one of its worst vindications. A cup match with Ipswich which had begun in the most violent, hostile atmosphere I have ever experienced inside a football ground was soon interrupted for eighteen minutes as the fighting on the terraces spilled on to the pitch. Thirty people had to be taken to hospital. The ground was closed for two matches, but after one match had been played at Portsmouth, the club's difficulty in finding anyone willing to play host led to the ban being relaxed. The escape from relegation was only temporary and the club fell back into the Third Division the following season.

This time there was no easy escape. Herbert Burnige was succeeded by Len Eppel as chairman and Peter Anderson replaced George Petchey as player–manager without a solution being found. As the club struggled in the lower half of the Third Division, the financial crisis became acute, as it did at so many clubs in the early eighties. Like most of them, Millwall found a rich businessman to succour them, and Alan Thorne took over as chairman. He did so with fighting words, saying that he expected Millwall's unenviable record of being the only London club (newcomers Wimbledon apart at that time) not to have reached the First Division to be quickly rectified. He also said that if the club's supporters did not behave themselves, he would not wait for the F A to close the club but would do so himself. Progress was slower than he had anticipated. In November 1982 Peter Anderson was sacked; he was eventually replaced by George Graham after Barry Kitchener's period as temporary manager in the interim in his last season with the club. Graham got the club back to the Second Division as runners-up to Bradford City in 1985 but left in the 1986 close season to join Arsenal as manager.

That success, however, was overshadowed by events off the field, just as so much of English football was overshadowed by the tragic events of 1985. Sadly, Millwall were again in the forefront of the traumas, their so-called fans erupting during a sixth round F A Cup match at Luton, where the game was interrupted for twenty-five minutes while they fought a pitched battle with police. National television coverage of the game brought it even greater attention than it might otherwise have had and produced serious government intervention for the first time – although the *Sun*, a paper not normally given to questioning Mrs Thatcher's motives, reported that her outrage had been fuelled by the fact that the riot kept reports of her latest diplomatic 'success' off the front pages.

Initially fined by the F A, they appealed successfully against the decision. How in any justice there could have been any other outcome is an unanswerable question, for to hold clubs or indeed the game responsible for the savagery of the thugs who wear their colours is indefensible, especially when much of the worst excesses, as at Luton, take place miles from the ground. To stress the point, at Luton the number of people there pretending to support Millwall exceeded the average home attendance at the Den, now sadly diminished from the days when Dunphy and his team-mates could count on a loyal 7 or 8,000. The club's name, however, had once again been dragged into the dirt.

Millwall People

Like Eamon, few of his team-mates found football glory elsewhere. The exception, perhaps predictably given footballers' frequent fallibility as judges, was Gordon Hill. For him, Millwall was a first step to greater things. He was transferred to Manchester United, then being reshaped by Tommy Docherty into one of the most thrilling if not reliable sides of the mid-seventies. He helped United to two Cup Finals, although he was substituted in both, and gained a Cup Winner's Medal and six England caps. He lost none of his chirpiness, informing the disbelieving United players that Dunphy had been the victim of the tennis joke when *Only a Game?* made the rounds of the United dressing-room. As at Millwall, his fellow professionals were less enamoured with his contribution than were the fans and manager, and once Dave Sexton replaced Docherty as United's manager Hill's Old Trafford career was short-lived. The parting was mutually abusive, Hill proclaiming that you needed 'A' levels to understand Sexton's tactics and Sexton saying that his winger was a very selfish player, and Hill followed Docherty to Derby. Their reunion was less fruitful, and as Derby declined, Docherty paid the penalty and Hill moved to America. His attempts to find a new English club as the bottom fell out of the American game were unsuccessful, but he returned to Europe anyway, spending the 1985-6 season with the Dutch First Division team Twente Enschede.

Bryan King and Alf Wood also reached the First Division, if

only fleetingly. King's progress was straightforward: he joined Coventry City in time for the 1975–6 season. But the move, sadly, was not to prove a success and an injury sustained soon after his move – one sustained, frustratingly, at home rather than on the football pitch – ended his career. Alf Wood's route to the First Division was less simple. He followed Dennis Burnett to Hull soon after Jago took over at the Den, subsequently joining Middlesbrough on a free transfer. He played twenty-two games and scored two goals for the First Division club, but his personal highlight was still ahead of him. At the end of his career he went to Wembley with Stafford Rangers in the 1979 FA Trophy Final, scoring both goals in their defeat of Kettering Town.

The other, much less central, figure in Dunphy's Millwall story to reach Wembley did so in rather more auspicious circumstances. Steve Sherwood, the goalkeeper on loan from Chelsea, moved to Watford after returning to Stamford Bridge and was in the team which lost to Everton in the 1984 Cup Final.

Barry Kitchener had no such high point in his career, but he battled on determinedly at the Den, surviving the ups and downs to set a new club appearance record of 523 Football League appearances by the time of his retirement in 1982.

For the rest, it was a story of decline, with only the speed and degree of the descent differing. Of the old team, Gordon Bolland stayed at Millwall until 1975 and then joined Boston in the Northern Premier League. Dennis Burnett found no satisfaction at Hull, briefly returned to Millwall on loan during Jago's first season and then moved to Brighton, where Peter Taylor too did not provide a set-up he could respect; he ended his career in America. Alan Dorney's stay at the club was stifled by the arrival of Jago's old player Tony Hazell, who followed his manager from QPR, and he moved to Dartford, Wimbledon's offer of terms to stay in the League coming a week too late.

Full-backs Bryan Brown and Harry Cripps both regained their places, temporarily at least. Brown's return was cut short by injury which ended his career. Harry moved to Charlton to join Eamon and help the side into the Second Division before he retired.

Brian Clark was also a survivor, moving on and down to Cardiff and Newport. Dougy Allder had a brief renaissance as a midfield player, Benny at one stage comparing him to Jim Baxter. He was unable to sustain his form, however, as injuries took their toll, and moves to Orient and Brentford did not revitalize his career. Frank Saul stayed with Millwall for another two seasons before joining Dagenham in the Isthmian League.

For the younger players, the fall from grace was even more rapid. Only Dave Donaldson went on to have a full Football League career, fighting off the challenge from one of Jago's first imports, the ex-Spurs player Ray Evans, and then moving on to play for Cambridge United in the Second Division. By 1985 his playing career had taken him to Hong Kong. Steve Brown, Eddie Jones and Ned Kelly failed to establish themselves and went into the Southern League.

Few of Dunphy's contemporaries are still in football. Harry Cripps, a survivor to the last, is Bobby Moore's coach at Southend after having had spells with Charlton and Crystal Palace. Bryan King has found a niche as a coach in Norway, where Dennis Burnett also worked briefly. Brian Clark had a short spell on the coaching staff at Cardiff before moving into industry, retaining his football connections by coaching a Cardiff amateur club. Billy Neill has outlasted everyone at Millwall, first on the football side and more recently as commercial manager. That side of the game also kept Alf Wood involved for a time with Birmingham City, but he left three years ago to set up his own promotions and marketing business in Birmingham, where he still is.

Dennis Burnett settled in Brighton, working as a taxi-driver, and Gordon Bolland settled in Boston, working as a rep. Barry Kitchener left East London and greengrocery, both surprisingly, to buy a shop in Caister. Alan Dorney works as a builder in South-East London and Bryan Brown took over a pub in Kent.

Benny Fenton stayed in football, but on the administrative side. After leaving Millwall he moved to Charlton as Secretary. He has now retired to the South Coast to live near his daughter, but he still keeps his hand in by scouting teams for a variety of clubs. Theo Foley is assistant manager at Arsenal, moving there last summer with George Graham after his second spell at the Den. He went there originally as Gordon Jago's assistant, replacing Lawrie Leslie, but left when Petchey replaced Jago. He was brought back by Graham in 1983. Lawrie Leslie survived Benny for a few months before leaving the club to work in schools as a coach.

Eamon's Predictions

It is often said that footballers make the worst tipsters, and Eamon's taste for overstating his case has occasionally led him into offering generous odds unwisely. But in the diary, as in his bets, he did come out about even. He was, of course, pretty accurate in his predictions for Millwall; his record with other clubs varied dramatically. He claims, with some justice, that his analysis of Carlisle, nineteenth in the Second Division when they visited Millwall in September, stands as one of the most outstanding pieces of analysis of all time, as they went on to gain promotion.

Against that can be balanced his assertion that Queen's Park Rangers would not last in the higher division. Instead, they consolidated their position successfully, and the following season missed the title by one point.

Wolves and West Ham, the other two First Division clubs encountered in pre-season, are less easily categorized. West Ham did indeed struggle in 1973–4, but over the following two seasons they won the Cup and then reached the final of the European Cup Winners' Cup before slipping down to the Second Division. Where do you draw the line?

The same question can be asked of Wolves. In 1973–4 they won the League Cup, which does little to support Eamon's reputation as an analyst, but it was a rare upsurge on a downward curve which has left them ultimately in their current parlous state.

In the Second Division Middlesbrough confirmed Eamon's good opinions. They eventually won the championship by fifteen points from Luton Town, and while Jack Charlton stayed in command they went on to establish themselves as a First Division team. His suspicion that Aston Villa's front players were not good enough to snatch goals on the break away from home was also correct. They managed fifteen away goals to finish two places below Millwall. Our disagreement (see pp. 171–6) about Sheffield Wednesday was also resolved in his favour. They ended the season eighteenth and were relegated the following year.

Preston, as their players had feared, were faced with a relegation battle, and lost it. They were joined by Crystal Palace, who did not find the Second Division 'no contest' as they had anticipated. Fulham, as Eamon expected, blew up to finish sandwiched between Millwall and Aston Villa. But, with Bobby Moore joining them in March, they had the basis of the team which went on to play West Ham in the 1975 Cup Final. A dramatic future also lay ahead for Nottingham Forest. Seventh that season, they were transformed by the arrival of Brian Clough two years later to begin a climb to claim the European Cup. Martin O'Neill and Ian Bowyer went with them all the way, to give renewed hope to every 'good pro'.

Index

of non-Millwall people and other clubs

READ MORE IN PENGUIN

In every corner of the world, on every subject under the sun, Penguin represents quality and variety – the very best in publishing today.

For complete information about books available from Penguin – including Puffins, Penguin Classics and Arkana – and how to order them, write to us at the appropriate address below. Please note that for copyright reasons the selection of books varies from country to country.

In the United Kingdom: Please write to *Dept. EP, Penguin Books Ltd, Bath Road, Harmondsworth, West Drayton, Middlesex UB7 0DA*

In the United States: Please write to *Consumer Sales, Penguin Putnam Inc., P.O. Box 12289 Dept. B, Newark, New Jersey 07101-5289.* VISA and MasterCard holders call 1-800-788-6262 to order Penguin titles

In Canada: Please write to *Penguin Books Canada Ltd, 10 Alcorn Avenue, Suite 300, Toronto, Ontario M4V 3B2*

In Australia: Please write to *Penguin Books Australia Ltd, P.O. Box 257, Ringwood, Victoria 3134*

In New Zealand: Please write to *Penguin Books (NZ) Ltd, Private Bag 102902, North Shore Mail Centre, Auckland 10*

In India: Please write to *Penguin Books India Pvt Ltd, 11 Community Centre, Panchsheel Park, New Delhi 110017*

In the Netherlands: Please write to *Penguin Books Netherlands bv, Postbus 3507, NL-1001 AH Amsterdam*

In Germany: Please write to *Penguin Books Deutschland GmbH, Metzlerstrasse 26, 60594 Frankfurt am Main*

In Spain: Please write to *Penguin Books S. A., Bravo Murillo 19, 1° B, 28015 Madrid*

In Italy: Please write to *Penguin Italia s.r.l., Via Benedetto Croce 2, 20094 Corsico, Milano*

In France: Please write to *Penguin France, Le Carré Wilson, 62 rue Benjamin Baillaud, 31500 Toulouse*

In Japan: Please write to *Penguin Books Japan Ltd, Kaneko Building, 2-3-25 Koraku, Bunkyo-Ku, Tokyo 112*

In South Africa: Please write to *Penguin Books South Africa (Pty) Ltd, Private Bag X14, Parkview, 2122 Johannesburg*

READ MORE IN PENGUIN

A CHOICE OF NON-FICTION

Time Out Film Guide Edited by John Pym

The definitive, up-to-the-minute directory of every aspect of world cinema from classics and silent epics to reissues and the latest releases.

Four-Iron in the Soul Lawrence Donegan

'A joy to read. Not since Bill Bryson plotted a random route through small-town America has such a breezy idea for a book had a happier (or funnier) result' *The Times*. 'Funny, beautifully observed and it tells you things about sport in general and golf in particular that nobody else thought to pass on' *Mail on Sunday*

Nelson Mandela: A Biography Martin Meredith

Nelson Mandela's role in delivering South Africa from racial division stands as one of the great triumphs of the twentieth century. In this brilliant account, Martin Meredith gives a vivid portrayal of the life and times of this towering figure. 'The best biography so far of Nelson Mandela' Raymond Whitaker, *Independent on Sunday*

In Search of Nature Edward O. Wilson

'*In Search of Nature* makes such stimulating reading that Edward O. Wilson might be regarded as a one-man recruitment bureau for tomorrow's biologists . . . His essays on ants tend to leave one gasping for breath, literally speaking . . . Yet he is equally enchanting in his accounts of sharks and snakes and New Guinea's birds of paradise' *The Times Higher Education Supplement*

Reflections on a Quiet Rebel Cal McCrystal

This extraordinary book is both a vivid memoir of Cal McCrystal's Irish Catholic childhood and a loving portrait of his father Charles, a 'quiet rebel' and unique man. 'A haunting book, lovely and loving. It explains more about one blighted corner of Ireland than a dozen dogged histories' *Scotsman*

READ MORE IN PENGUIN

A CHOICE OF NON-FICTION

Falling Leaves Adeline Yen Mah

'I am still haunted by Mah's memoir ... Riveting. A marvel of memory. Poignant proof of the human will to endure' Amy Tan. *'Falling Leaves* is a terrible and riveting family history ... It is also a story about endurance and the cost it can exact' *Daily Telegraph*

Anatomy of a Miracle Patti Waldmeir

The peaceful birth of black majority rule in South Africa has been seen by many as a miracle – or at least political magic. 'Essential reading for anyone interested in South Africa' *Literary Review*. 'One of the most authoritative reporters on the South African scene ... her analytical skills are deadly' *Sunday Times*

My Name Escapes Me Alec Guinness

'His diary for the eighteen months from January 1995 to June 1996 is a book of immense charm and the source of almost undiluted pleasure. Imagine a lucky dip where each entry comes up with a prize and you will have some measure of the writing' *Daily Mail*

The Feminization of Nature Deborah Cadbury

Scientists around the world are uncovering alarming changes in human reproduction and health. There is strong evidence that sperm counts have fallen dramatically. Testicular and prostate cancer are on the increase. Different species are showing signs of 'feminization' or even 'changing sex'. 'Grips you from page one ... it reads like a Michael Crichton thriller' John Gribbin

The Portuguese Marion Kaplan

This book records Portugal's rich and turbulent history and also ranges lightly across the issues, incongruities and paradoxes of Portugal today. 'Sympathetic, perceptive, lively and full of information' *The Times Literary Supplement*

READ MORE IN PENGUIN

A CHOICE OF NON-FICTION

Racers Richard Williams

'Where Williams really scores is in his evocation of the political chicanery and secret vendettas in Formula One' *Guardian*. 'Gets under the skin of this intelligent, sophisticated and cold-blooded sport ... the plot grips like Pirellis on a rain-slicked mountain pass' *Observer*

Floyd on Africa Keith Floyd

Keith Floyd's wonderful chronicle of cooking, eating and travelling around Zambia, Zimbabwe, Madagascar and South Africa is part safari and part recipe book. Inspired by the tropical fruits in the markets, the fish from sparkling lakes and the game from the bush, he conjures up some unforgettable meals.

The Way to Write John Fairfax and John Moat

While of direct use to the more practised writer, *The Way to Write* remains alive to the difficulties experienced by those who would like to explore their own creative writing but feel unsure of how to begin. This stimulating book takes you from the first confrontation with the blank page to the final manuscript.

The Little Book of Calm Paul Wilson

Feeling stressed? Need some help to regain balance in your life? The bestselling *The Little Book of Calm* is full of advice to follow and thoughts to inspire. Open it at any page and you will find a path to inner peace.

American Frontiers Gregory H. Nobles

'At last someone has written a narrative of America's frontier experience with sensitivity and insight This is a book which will appeal to both the specialist and the novice' James M. McPherson, Princeton University

READ MORE IN PENGUIN

A CHOICE OF NON-FICTION

The Old Patagonian Express Paul Theroux

Beginning his journey in Boston, where he boarded the subway commuter train, Paul Theroux travelled the length of North and South America, to his destination in Patagonia. 'Fascinating, beautifully written ... a vivid travelogue described with the sensitive, richly observant pen of a born writer' *Sunday Express*

The Lions Diary Jeremy Guscott with Nick Cain

Packed with action from the pitch, the dressing-room and the heartlands, *The Lions Diary* is the complete insiders' account of the most successful tour in British rugby history. 'Hugely entertaining. If you want a book that tells it from the inside of a sweaty tracksuit after endless shuttle-runs, this is the one' *Daily Telegraph*

Michael Heseltine Michael Crick

'Michael Crick confirms his reputation as a superb investigator. He writes wittily and engagingly with a mastery of narrative pace as well as a shrewd political nose ... it should prove the definitive life' *The Times Literary Supplement*. 'Entertaining ... seems set to become the standard tome on his subject' *The Times*

Mornings in the Dark Edited by David Parkinson
The Graham Greene Film Reader

Prompted by 'a sense of fun' and 'that dangerous third Martini' at a party in June 1935, Graham Greene volunteered himself as the *Spectator* film critic. 'His film reviews are among the most trenchant, witty and memorable one is ever likely to read' *Sunday Times*

Fenland Chronicle Sybil Marshall

In *Fenland Chronicle* Sybil Marshall has collected together her mother's and father's remembrances of their childhood, marriage, family life and work in this traditional corner of England and drawn them into a vivid portrait of a time gone by.

BILL WALLACE

Award-winning author Bill Wallace brings you fun-filled
animal stories full of humor and exciting adventures.

BEAUTY

RED DOG*

TRAPPED IN DEATH CAVE*

A DOG CALLED KITTY

DANGER ON PANTHER PEAK

SNOT STEW

**FERRET IN THE BEDROOM,
LIZARDS IN THE FRIDGE**

DANGER IN QUICKSAND SWAMP

THE CHRISTMAS SPURS

TOTALLY DISGUSTING!

BUFFALO GAL

NEVER SAY QUIT

BIGGEST KLUTZ IN FIFTH GRADE

BLACKWATER SWAMP

WATCHDOG AND THE COYOTES

TRUE FRIENDS

JOURNEY INTO TERROR

THE FINAL FREEDOM

THE BACKWARD BIRD DOG

UPCHUCK AND THE ROTTEN WILLY

**UPCHUCK AND THE ROTTEN WILLY:
THE GREAT ESCAPE**

**UPCHUCK AND THE ROTTEN WILLY:
RUNNING WILD**

THE FLYING FLEA, CALLIE, AND ME

ALOHA SUMMER

CHOMPS, FLEA,, AND GRAY CAT (THAT'S ME)!

BUB MOOSE

A MINSTREL® BOOK

Published by Pocket Books

648-34